CIVIL WAR BLOCKADE RUNNING ON THE TEXAS COAST

CIVIL WAR BLOCKADE RUNNING ON THE TEXAS COAST

ANDREW W. HALL

THE
History
PRESS

Published by The History Press
Charleston, SC 29403
www.historypress.net

First published 2014

ISBN 978-1-5402-2473-6

Library of Congress CIP data applied for.

For Becki, Faith and Emily Faith

CONTENTS

ACKNOWLEDGEMENTS

This volume had its genesis in 1995 when I got a phone call from my colleague Casey Greene at the archives at Rosenberg Library in Galveston. Casey had a patron from out of town who was looking for more information on a specific Civil War blockade runner wrecked here in 1865. The archives didn't have much information on the subject, but Casey thought I might be able to help the patron. I didn't have much on the ship either, but I said I'd be happy to share what I could.

The visitor was a physician from Charleston, South Carolina, named Charles Peery. Dr. Peery made his living as a gynecologic surgeon, but his passion was the Civil War and blockade running, especially in and around his hometown. He was in Houston for a medical conference but played hooky from it that day to come to Galveston to see if he could find out more about the wreck of the famous blockade runner *Denbigh*, burned off the Bolivar Peninsula in May 1865. My nautical archaeologist friend Tom Oertling and I, with our wives, Sarita and Rebecca, spent a long evening together talking shipwrecks and history over dinner and nautical charts with Peery before he got back in his rental car and headed for his hotel in Houston. As we parted, Peery handed Tom and me each one of his business cards. "Call me at that number," he said. "They won't let you talk to me, but tell them it's about the Civil War, and they'll come get me out of surgery." I believe to this day that he was dead serious about that last part.

Nothing came of Dr. Peery's visit for more than a year, but it did put *Denbigh* on the map for each of us, at least mentally. Tom found it on the map literally in the fall of 1996 while reviewing a chart from the 1880s for another project. The chart bore a carefully inscribed dot off the Bolivar Peninsula with the notation "WRECK *DENBIGH*." The chart was not marked with latitude and longitude, but it did show the location of the then-new Bolivar Lighthouse, a structure that still stands today. By measuring carefully the bearing and distance on the nineteenth-century chart from the lighthouse to the position marked as the wreck, it was possible to plot those coordinates on a modern chart with some precision.

On a very cold day not long before Christmas 1996, Tom and our longtime colleague Barto Arnold, from the Institute of Nautical Archaeology at Texas A&M, donned wetsuits and traveled by motorboat to the position we'd calculated. The water was only fifty degrees Fahrenheit, but it didn't matter—they quickly recognized the distinctive, circular iron frames of the ship's paddlewheels and enormous, box-like boiler. *Denbigh* was no longer a lost wreck.

Barto, Tom and I went on to work with the Institute of Nautical Archaeology's *Denbigh* Project for the next several years. Blockade running during the Civil War has remained an interest of mine ever since. A great many folks have provided assistance and encouragement along the way. First among these is Barto, who gave me the opportunity to take on a substantive role with the project, on which I was able to do much of the early historical research, as well as public education programming and illustration work. In the years since, Barto has shepherded the project to be the most comprehensive study done of a Confederate blockade runner from the Civil War.

My fellow co-principal investigator on the project, Tom Oertling, has been an ongoing source of support and guidance even after our work together on the project ended. Others from the *Denbigh* Project who have been helpful in this journey include engineer Gene Shimko, researcher Jerry Williams and divers Eric Van Velzen and Alex Hazlett. Sam Ernst and Andrew Wiggins, naval architecture and marine engineering students at the Webb Institute who spent a summer working on the project, later used that experience in developing a technological history of blockade runners that contributes to this work.

The Galveston and Texas History Center at Rosenberg Library in Galveston has been invaluable. In addition to former head of special collections Casey Greene, other Rosenberg staffers who have assisted with this research include current head of special collections Peggy Dillard, Mary Magdalena Hernandez, Travis Bible, Jenna de Graffenried, Julia Dunn, Shelly Kelly and Anna Peebler. A special note of thanks goes to archivist

Carol Wood, who has been an enthusiastic and engaged supporter. The staff of the Brazoria County Historical Museum, in particular Michael Bailey and Herb Boykin, have also been generous with their time and source material. The crew at the Civil War Talk online forum, including David L. Bright, Mark F. Jenkins, Peter Joseph, J.W. Wallis and Kazimierz Zygadlo, have been a good sounding board and source for additional information. My friend Richard Eisenhour, an incorrigible collector of historical ephemera, providently shared with me the card from Hendley's Lookout that I believe is published here for the first time.

In addition to archival research, much of my understanding and appreciation of blockade running has come from close examination and investigation of period shipwrecks. Through affiliation with the Texas Historical Commission, the Institute of Nautical Archaeology, the PAST Foundation, the Southwest Underwater Archaeology Society and the NOAA Maritime Heritage Program, I've had the opportunity to dive on, record or help interpret several Civil War–era shipwrecks, four of which—*Denbigh*, *Will o' the Wisp*, USS *Hatteras* and *Tonawanda* (ex-USS *Arkansas*)—played roles in the blockade in Texas.

I want to thank my friend Edward T. Cotham Jr., author of *Battle on the Bay: The Civil War Struggle for Galveston* and other works, for his persistent encouragement and well-considered guidance. My fellow Civil War blogger and friend James M. Schmidt has been a valuable sounding board for this work, based both on his experience as an author and his knowledge of Galveston in the mid-nineteenth century. I would like to extend a special note of thanks to Amy Borgens, Barto Arnold, Tom Oertling and Frank Hole for reviewing specific parts of the manuscript and suggesting changes as needed. The final work is better because of their contributions.

Finally, this work would not exist without the patience and guidance of my editors at The History Press, Christen Thompson and Will Collicott. They and the rest of the staff at The History Press provided encouragement, guidance and the benefit of their experience throughout this process. They make me look good.

Chapter 1
KING COTTON

I have seen many things that you all have not seen. The thousands of immigrants who'd be glad to fight for the Yankees for food and a few dollars, the factories, the foundries, the shipyards, the iron and coal mines—all the things we haven't got. Why, all we have is cotton and slaves and arrogance.
—*Rhett Butler, in Margaret Mitchell's* Gone with the Wind

On the eve of the American Civil War, the Texas coast was booming, standing as the gateway between the expansive United States and the southwestern frontier. A majority of the goods and people moving in and out of Texas came by sea, which was generally faster, more comfortable and cheaper than traveling overland.

It was not always this way. The Spanish rulers of Texas, and the Mexican governments that succeeded them after 1820, did not view the coast and inland waterways in the same way that the Americans would later. Spanish settlements and outposts, largely confined to the southern and western parts of the region, did not rely significantly on waterways for transport. The Spanish failed to establish any port of significance along what is now the Texas coast; communications between Spanish settlements depended entirely on a series of trails, the most famous of which was *el Camino Real* (the Royal Road) extending from Monclova and Saltillo, in present-day Mexico, through San Antonio to Nacogdoches in far East Texas.[1]

During its short rule over Texas (1821–36), the Mexican government made a critical change in policy that ultimately would cause it to lose control over the province altogether: it opened the door to colonization in Texas, notably by allowing Stephen F. Austin to found a colony at San Felipe on the Brazos River.[2] Austin's settlers, and those who came after them, would very quickly establish the coast and navigable rivers as the primary and essential means of transportation in what would become Anglo-American Texas.

The Anglo settlers that moved into Texas after Mexico won its independence from Spain brought a new way of doing things. Austin's colony was centered near the coast along the watersheds of the Brazos and Colorado Rivers, south of present-day Houston. These immigrants to Texas, mostly from the southern United States, transplanted with them a plantation culture centered largely on the cultivation of cotton and sugar as cash crops. This required a far more efficient transportation infrastructure than the Spanish had built, along with all the other elements of commerce that go with it—warehousing, banking, insurance, commission agents and many others.

Austin's colony built a small port settlement at the mouth of the Brazos River called Velasco, but it left much to be desired. Access to the river itself was limited to only the lightest-draft vessels, and there was no sheltered anchorage at all. Ships calling at Velasco were obliged to anchor off the beach, exposed to the currents and surf of the Gulf of Mexico. A few miles up the coast, though, Galveston Island offered the best natural harbor in the region. Galveston had been settled by a series of adventurers in the early years of the century, including the pirate Jean Laffite. Galveston could accommodate the larger classes of ships that plied the Gulf of Mexico. Galveston Harbor, a long, narrow waterway running parallel to the shore on the bay side of the island, was twenty or more feet deep for most of its length. Long wooden piers were built out from the shore on the bay side into the deeper water, with wharves built at right angles to them (i.e., parallel to the harbor and the shore), allowing deep-draft vessels to tie up directly at the wharf to load and unload passengers and cargo. Over time, these T-headed piers were gradually connected to one another, forming a continuous set of wharf frontage. The shallow water behind the line of wharf frontage was gradually filled in, creating the Galveston waterfront that survives today.

The eastern end of Galveston Island curves northward, making a sort of fishhook shape pointing up into Galveston Bay. The tip of the hook commands an unobstructed view of the entrance to the bay and, from the earliest days of settlement on the island, was the site of a military post of one sort or another. Inevitably, this geographic feature came to be known as

Fort Point, a name it retains today, and the battery there would become a key defensive position during the Civil War. Between Fort Point and the end of the Bolivar Peninsula, something over two miles away to the northeast, lies an open expanse of water where Galveston Bay meets the Gulf of Mexico. This wide area, continually scoured by the ebb and flow of the tide between the bay and the Gulf, is deep and forms an open anchorage.

As a port, Galveston had competition on the coast. In the mid-1840s, the town of Indianola was founded on Matagorda Bay, about one hundred miles farther south along the coast from Galveston. Indianola was originally envisioned as a landing place for German immigrants sponsored by the *Adelsverein*, or the German Immigration Company, headed for settlements on what was then the western frontier of Texas. Indianola would grow beyond those origins over the next four decades, becoming an important secondary port on the Texas coast, but was abandoned after being largely destroyed by hurricanes in 1875 and 1886.

Galveston, though, remained the preeminent port in Texas. In addition to the advantages of its natural harbor, the island stands at the mouth of Galveston Bay, a broad, open expanse of water into which empties both the Trinity River and Buffalo Bayou. The Trinity was navigable for many miles upstream into the eastern part of the state, while Buffalo Bayou provided access by riverboat to Houston, founded soon after the Texas Revolution with the promise to become "the great commercial emporium of Texas." By 1860, railroads fanned out from Houston in all directions, providing convenient transportation of people and goods farther into the Texas interior.

Texas's booming economy, like most of the country's in 1860, was built on the back of slave labor. It had been so for four decades. When the newly established Mexican government opened Texas to settlement by Austin's colonists in the 1820s, many of the settlers brought with them slaves to work the land, claiming that they were merely "servants" to get around the Mexican government's nominal prohibition of chattel bondage. The settlement of slaveholders with their bondsmen and the development of a plantation culture along the Colorado, Brazos and Trinity Rivers intensified after Texas won its independence from Mexico in 1836. Texas quickly gained a reputation as "a virtual empire for slavery" through its years as a republic and early U.S. statehood. Texas's slave population grew at a faster rate than its free population did; the number of enslaved persons more than tripled between 1850 and 1860, largely due to southern slaveholders swarming into the state where good land was plentiful and cheap. At the same time, Texas adopted some of the most stringent laws in the South

The Federal Blockade of the
Western Gulf of Mexico

0   50 kilometers

0   50 statute miles

0   50 nautical miles

Houston

Sabine Pass

Galveston

Velasco

Pass Cavallo

Aransas Pass

GULF OF M[exico]

Distances Between Selected Ports:

Galveston and Havana
754 nautical miles, 94 hours at 8 knots
Mobile and Havana
540 nautical miles, 68 hours at 8 knots
Bagdad and Havana
830 nautical miles, 104 hours at 8 knots
Galveston and Vera Cruz
610 nautical miles, 77 hours at 8 knots

Brownsville

Bagdad

Matamoros

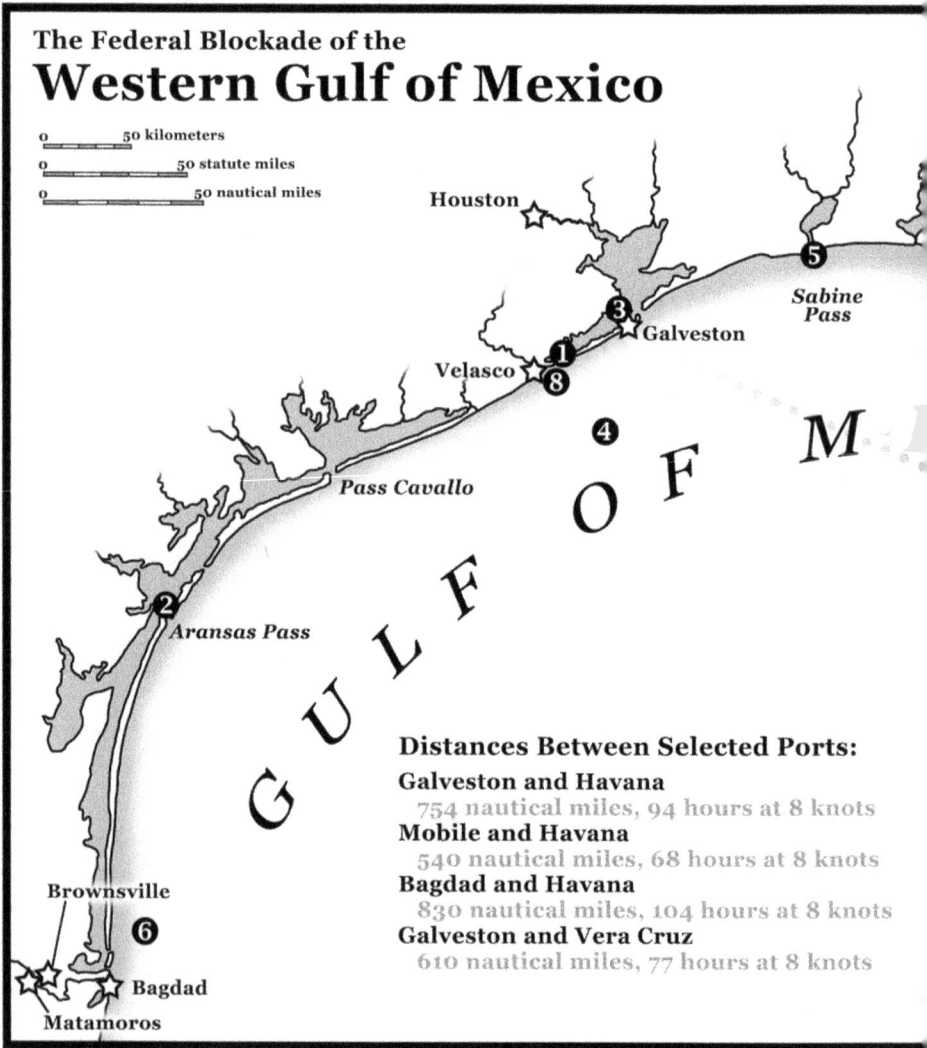

The Federal blockade in the Western Gulf of Mexico, 1861–65. *Original map by the author.*

restricting the presence and activities of free black persons. Free African Americans were almost nonexistent in Texas on the eve of the Civil War; the 1860 U.S. Census recorded just 355 "free colored persons" in the entire state, making up only about two-tenths of 1 percent of the total number of African Americans in Texas.[3]

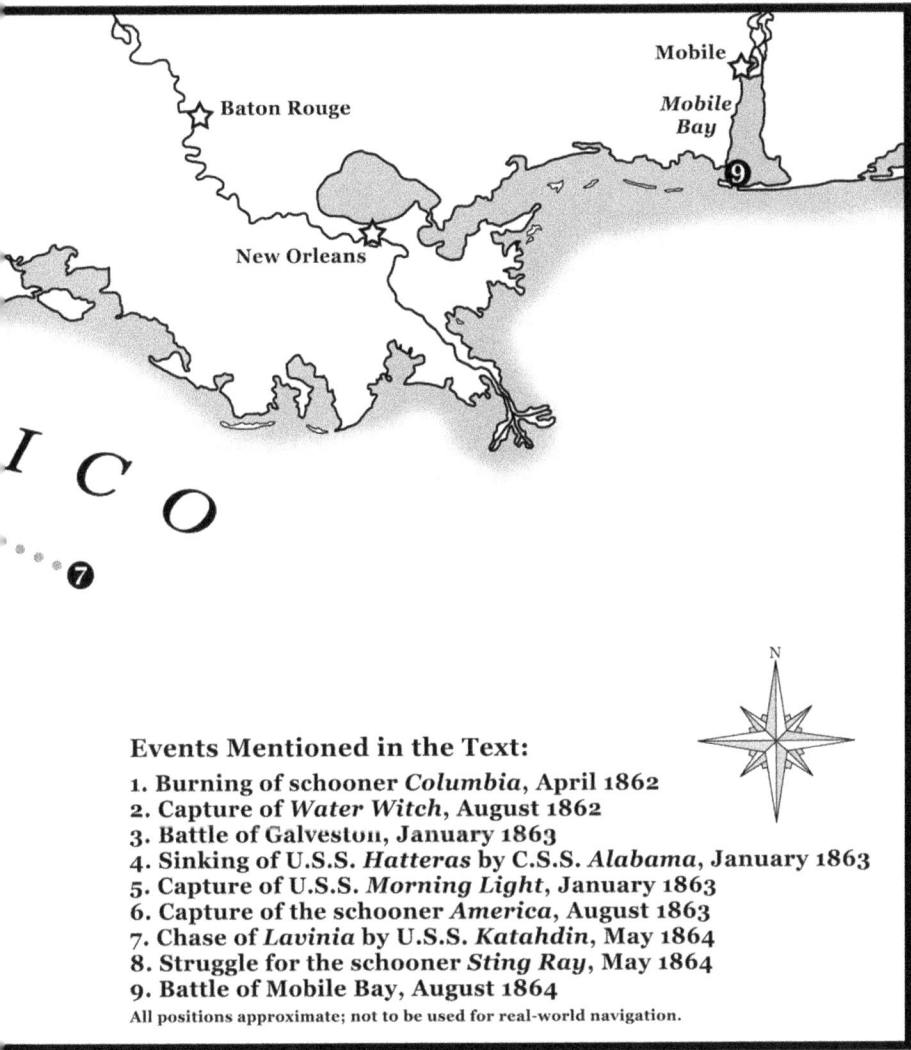

Events Mentioned in the Text:

1. Burning of schooner *Columbia*, April 1862
2. Capture of *Water Witch*, August 1862
3. Battle of Galveston, January 1863
4. Sinking of U.S.S. *Hatteras* by C.S.S. *Alabama*, January 1863
5. Capture of U.S.S. *Morning Light*, January 1863
6. Capture of the schooner *America*, August 1863
7. Chase of *Lavinia* by U.S.S. *Katahdin*, May 1864
8. Struggle for the schooner *Sting Ray*, May 1864
9. Battle of Mobile Bay, August 1864

All positions approximate; not to be used for real-world navigation.

The engine that drove this plantation culture, of course, was cotton. Cotton shipments from Galveston and other Texas ports rose steadily from 31,806 five-hundred-pound bales in 1850 to just under a quarter million bales in 1860, an increase of nearly 700 percent in just over a decade. A slim majority of this cotton was shipped to other U.S. ports in what was termed the "coastwise" trade, while about 45 percent of it in 1860 was loaded onto ships bound overseas. Roughly a third of the cotton shipped out of Texas in 1860 was bound for the United Kingdom. (The cotton shipping season that year had been extraordinarily lucrative, filling warehouses in Liverpool and Manchester with the white staple. This fact would prove to be a serious liability for the South when it later sought to use European demand for cotton as leverage to win diplomatic recognition for the Confederacy.) Texas enjoyed a staggeringly lopsided trade balance in 1860, with imports coming into Galveston directly from foreign ports valued at only $544,000, against foreign exports shipped from Galveston topping well over $6 million.[4]

On the eve of secession, then, Texas stood astride the frontier on the west and the Deep South to the east. Its new cities, particularly Galveston and Houston, were mercantile boomtowns, catering to the movement of people and cargoes between the interior of the state to the rest of the United States and beyond. That would all come crashing to a halt in the first months of 1861 as the nation tore itself apart over the future of slavery.

Chapter 2

THE BLOCKADE AT LAST!

An effective blockade of the port of Galveston, Texas has been established.
—*Flag Officer William Mervine, U.S. Navy*

At four thirty on the morning of Friday, April 12, 1861, the predawn stillness over Charleston was pierced by flash and thunder as batteries manned by secessionist militia opened fire on Fort Sumter, a squat, five-sided brick strongpoint that guarded the entrance to the harbor. South Carolina had declared its secession from the Union almost four months before, and the presence of a U.S. military garrison at Charleston—first at Fort Moultrie, on the mainland, and then evacuated to Fort Sumter—had become an increasingly contentious issue for the Palmetto State and the others that had followed it out of the Union. Abraham Lincoln's election as president in November 1860, along with his so-called "Black Republican" party's explicit platform to stop the spread of slavery to new states and territories in the West, had been the final event that pushed the fire-eating secessionists in South Carolina to action, declaring themselves seceded from the United States. Now, the newly inaugurated U.S. president was on the verge of resupplying the small garrison holed up at Sumter and reinforcing their number, a move that would make Sumter virtually impregnable for months to come. Caught between an increasingly agitated secessionist public demanding the excision of U.S. military forces from South Carolina and the prospect of the U.S. Major Robert Anderson and his reinforced garrison remaining at Sumter indefinitely, the secessionists chose to act. The concussion of that first shell detonating over Sumter would reverberate for the next four years.

Lincoln had come into office hoping to avoid a military confrontation over secession and perhaps convince the seceded states to return to the Union. Though he personally had always found the institution of slavery abhorrent, he saw abolition and emancipation as something beyond the legitimate reach of federal authority. He also viewed the preservation of the Union as a higher goal than ending chattel bondage where it currently existed, and to that end, he indicated in his inaugural address on March 4 that he had "no objection" to a constitutional amendment, put forward by Representative Thomas Corwin of Ohio, that would perpetuate slavery in the U.S. Constitution indefinitely. Corwin's proposed amendment was a last-ditch effort to bring the seven already-seceded states back into the Union, but it was too late; they would not re-enter the Union on their own volition.

Once Fort Sumter had been fired upon, it became clear that restoring the Union would require military force to put down what the administration viewed as an armed rebellion. North and South, events began to move quickly. On April 15, the day after Major Anderson surrendered Sumter to the Confederacy, Lincoln called for seventy-five thousand volunteers for three months' service to put down the rebellion. Virginia passed an ordinance of secession on April 17, and three days later, Virginia militiamen seized the navy yard at Norfolk, depriving the U.S. Navy of one of its primary construction, repair and depot facilities.

On the same day that Virginia passed its ordinance of secession, April 17, Confederate president Jefferson Davis issued a proclamation calling on southern citizens to apply for "letters of marque" authorizing them to attack Union shipping on behalf of the Confederate national government.[5] This was an explicit war act. Privateering had a long history among Western nations and was often used to great effect by a weaker maritime power against a stronger one. A letter of marque authorized private citizens to outfit, man and arm their own vessels and use them to capture or destroy enemy shipping and keep the profits. The major European powers had formally sworn off privateering in the Treaty of Paris of 1856, declaring the practice to be illegal and amounting to piracy. The United States, perhaps mindful of the role American privateering had played in the American Revolution and the War of 1812, had not signed the treaty. Now the new U.S. president found himself facing the prospect of having to deal with privateers seeking out American shipping on the high seas. Lincoln quietly let European governments know that even though the United States had never signed the treaty, his administration would nonetheless observe it in practice and not issue letters of marque to privateers.

Jefferson Davis's call for Confederate privateers, though, had other consequences because it freed Lincoln's hand to meet force with force. On April 19, 1861—the eighty-sixth anniversary of the Battles of Lexington and Concord that sparked the American Revolution—Lincoln issued Proclamation No. 81, "Declaring a Blockade of Ports in Rebellious States." The proclamation stated that "a competent force will be posted so as to prevent entrance and exit of vessels from the ports aforesaid" in South Carolina, Georgia, Alabama, Florida, Mississippi, Louisiana and Texas and that any vessel attempting to violate the blockade would be stopped and warned off by U.S. naval vessels. Any vessel caught attempting to pass the blockade a second time "will be captured and sent to the nearest convenient port for such proceedings against her and her cargo as prize."[6] Virginia and North Carolina were added to the blockade list eight days later, extending the Union blockade from the Virginia Capes at the entrance to Chesapeake Bay to the sluggish mouth of the Rio Grande at the border with Mexico.[7]

As a matter of law, Lincoln's blockade of the South was a dubious prospect. The strict legality of the blockade, as recognized by international custom and treaty at the time, remains a hotly debated topic more than a century and a half later.[8] A blockade of an enemy's ports had long been recognized as a legitimate means of warfare. The United Kingdom, the world's preeminent maritime power at the time, had used a blockade strategy to great effect against the French during the Napoleonic Wars and against the Americans during the War of 1812. But international convention held blockading to be a technique used *between nations*, not between different parts of the *same nation*, in order to be recognized and honored by the international community. This ran counter to the core principle that governed Union strategy throughout the war—that the Confederacy was a not a legitimate government but a "legal fiction," and that the southern states remained part of the greater United States, but temporarily in a state of rebellion or insurrection. Both Secretary of the Navy Gideon Welles and Senator Charles Sumner advised Lincoln against declaring a blockade, arguing that a blockade was recognized as an act of war between belligerent nations and that establishing one would be granting legitimacy to the Confederacy. Instead, Welles and Sumner urged Lincoln simply to use his authority as president to announce those ports as closed to foreign commerce. Lincoln rejected this approach, believing (as was ultimately proved even under blockade) that foreign shipping would not be deterred by such a policy.[9] Lincoln's declaration and establishment of a blockade of southern ports, while still refusing to recognize or treat the Confederate States as a foreign power, was one facet of a legalistic conundrum that the administration would struggle with over the next four years: finding a way to deal with the de facto Confederate government in Richmond and the United States' diplomatic contacts overseas (particularly the British) on myriad issues without ever formally acknowledging the Confederacy as a legitimate nation.

As the crisis over secession and Fort Sumter grew, Lincoln and his advisors gave a lot of thought to how they would respond if there were to be a military confrontation. Lincoln had no background in international affairs or the so-called law of nations, but he understood the core issues well enough to know that he was out of his depth in trying to make his case for the blockade to Britain

U.S. secretary of the navy Gideon Welles. *National Archives.*

and France. This job he relegated to his secretary of state, William Seward, who was given the task of convincing the European powers not to challenge a Union blockade of Confederate ports if secession and the then-simmering dispute over Fort Sumter boiled over into armed conflict.

On March 20, Seward called on Lord Lyons, the British ambassador to the United States, to sound him out on his government's reaction if the United States took action to "interrupt" foreign commerce with southern ports. Lyons understood this to be coded talk for a blockade and somewhat rashly threatened that, in response, the British government would likely grant diplomatic recognition to the Confederacy, a move that would both acknowledge the Confederate States as a sovereign power and raise the prospect of the Royal Navy's intervention to keep its trade with the South open. These outcomes were ones that the Lincoln administration needed

Lord Lyons, British ambassador to the United States. *Library of Congress.*

desperately to avoid, but Seward's clumsy approach to Lyons had laid them bare on the diplomatic table.[10]

Both men had said too much at their meeting on March 20, but Seward made matters much worse the following evening when he attended a dinner party hosted by Lyons that was also attended by the ministers of the other major European nations. There, Seward floated the idea of stationing U.S. naval vessels off the main southern ports so that they could stop inbound foreign shipping and collect import tariffs at sea before those vessels ever reached the dock. The monies collected in this way would be small, given that even the largest southern ports collected a tiny fraction of the revenues generated by northern ports like New York and Boston. But the practice would be an explicit and unmistakable demonstration of the United States' continued, unbroken sovereignty over that essential government function. (It was also not a new idea, having been proposed but not acted upon by the Jackson administration during the Nullification Crisis nearly three decades before.) Despite Seward's repeated assurance that such an arrangement would be something other than a blockade, the other ambassadors saw his position as a distinction without a difference. It also didn't help that Seward—"lubricated and loquacious" after a fine meal at which the champagne flowed freely—made a spectacle of himself, loudly haranguing the French and Russian ambassadors to share with him copies of instructions their governments had sent their consuls in the southern states. When Lyons stepped into the conversation to try to calm things, Seward angrily made the same demand of him, too. It was an ugly scene, of a sort rarely witnessed at diplomatic dinner parties. Seward's proposal for tariff collection at sea found no support and, more important, diminished the foreign ambassadors' view of the competency of the new president and his senior advisors. Seward's "lubricated" behavior also reinforced the diplomats' worst stereotypes of Americans as boorish, arrogant neophytes demanding respect and deference from established European powers that they had not earned.[11]

For weeks after Lincoln's proclamation of the blockade, things in Galveston and Texas remained much as they had been. The cotton shipping season was already past, and few large, seagoing ships could be seen in the harbor. The prospects of a Union blockade was a frequent topic of discussion in the local press, but the printed editorials—often copied from Southern-leaning papers elsewhere—reflected a supreme confidence that even if a blockade came to pass, European intervention would quickly raise it. "The blockade question…cannot be solved by any government in America," the *Galveston Civilian and Gazette* printed on June 11, repeating a piece originally from the *London Telegraph*, "but must be left to the maritime powers of Europe…President Lincoln has the interests of the Union to protect and [Prime Minister] Lord Palmerston is bound to defend those of Great Britain, but the former cannot be allowed to blockade our flag out of Southern ports, or the latter [be] stimulated by any partisan advocacy of

U.S. secretary of state William Seward. *National Archives.*

Northern ambition." Others were dismissive. The *Beaumont Banner* argued that "if Lincoln's proclamations were equivalent to large and well appointed fleets, we would be in a bad way [in] a short time, but as he hasn't one good ship for each hundred miles of coast he has declared to be strictly blockaded, we are rather disposed to be mirthful." The *Banner* went on to predict that there would be no blockade, at least not before mid-September.[12]

On Strand Street in Galveston, volunteers organized a watch on the rooftop of one of the tallest buildings in the city, Hendley's Row. The cupola atop the easternmost section of the structure had an unobstructed view of

Galveston Bay to the north, the entrance to Galveston Bay to the northeast and the Gulf of Mexico to the east and south. The volunteers took to their work with enthusiasm, setting up a flagpole on the roof and making regular entries in a logbook of their observations. They referred to themselves as the JOLOs; no one today seems to know the meaning of those initials, although it's presumed that the last two words were "look outs."

Like so many during that spring of 1861 in both the North and South, the JOLOs seem to have reveled in the excitement of the coming conflict. They worked out a code of warning signals to be flown from what they dubbed the "Hendley Watch Tower" or the "Hendley Lookout" and posted copies around town so that citizens could read them. They fitted out the cupola with two large telescopes "of great power," as well as numerous hand-held spyglasses. The JOLOs clearly enjoyed their new prominence as guardians of the coast, and the cupola became a popular spot for curious visitors. With "politeness and attention" on the part of the watchmen, the local newspaper reported, the tower became "quite a fashionable place of resort both day and evening." When not entertaining visitors, the JOLOs fought off boredom by making like pirates and capturing "prizes"—like a water cooler to make their accommodations more comfortable—from nearby merchants.[13]

Then, on Tuesday morning, July 2, the JOLOs spotted two new vessels, one of them clearly a warship, coming up over the horizon. They promptly hoisted a red flag, the signal for an enemy vessel, and below it pennants signifying the sighting of both a steamship and a sailing vessel. As word of the sighting spread, Galvestonians clambered up onto rooftops, and widows' walks atop some of the grander houses, in hopes of catching a glimpse of the new arrivals.

The steamship was USS *South Carolina*, built as a civilian merchant vessel to operate on the Atlantic seaboard, carrying passengers and cargo between Savannah, Charleston, Norfolk and Boston. *South Carolina* was, in fact, one of the first civilian steamers acquired by the U.S. Navy and outfitted for wartime service. Her armament, scraped together from what was immediately at hand, at this time consisted of four eight-inch smoothbore guns and a single forty-two-pounder gun on a pivot. Nonetheless, it was sufficient for service off the Texas coast, where she would be unlikely to encounter a Confederate warship.[14]

After *South Carolina* anchored off the bar, she hoisted a flag calling for a local pilot to come on board, the standard signal for a ship intending to enter the harbor. A local pilot, Thomas Chubb, sailed out in the schooner *Royal*

Advertising card for Hendley's Lookout. *Rosenberg Library via Richard Eisenhour.*

Yacht, along with prominent local citizen J. S. Sydnor. The captain of *South Carolina,* Commander James Alden, received Chubb and Sydnor "with due ceremony and marked politeness" and handed Sydnor written notice from the commanding officer of the U.S. Navy's Gulf Blockading Squadron that Galveston was now formally under blockade:

> *I, William Mervine, flag officer, commanding the United States naval forces comprising the Gulf squadron, give notice that, by virtue of the authority and power in me vested, and in pursuance of the proclamation of His Excellency the President of the United States, promulgated under date of April 19 and 27, 1861, respectively, that an effective blockade of the port of Galveston, Texas has been established, and will be rigidly enforced and maintained against all vessels (public armed vessels of foreign powers alone excepted) which attempt to enter or depart from said port.[15]*

Alden, Chubb and Sydnor talked for about an hour. Alden took a respectful but firm tone, expressing regret that relations between the northern and southern states had come to this point but assuring the Galveston men that he believed the Union had the strength to "bring the southern states into subjection," if necessary, and that he would do his duty as a naval officer in

Commander James Alden of USS *South Carolina* (postwar image). *Porter's* Naval History of the Civil War.

that regard even if it included shelling the city. Chubb and Sydnor asserted in return that the whole populace supported secession and "would suffer extermination" rather than be returned to the Union by force of arms. Chubb, upon learning that he and Alden both had grown up in Charlestown, Massachusetts, offered himself as evidence that "all our citizens of southern, northern, as well as foreign origin, are determined to fight to the last sooner than submit to the detestable rule of Lincoln."[16]

For all the serious posturing, though, the men appear to have kept the talk friendly enough on the surface, even "jocular." Strained, double-entendre jokes seem to have been part of the conversation. Before the Confederates left his ship, Alden commented that he'd heard "fish" were plentiful on the Texas coast and that he hoped to catch some. Chubb and Sydnor replied, in studied earnestness, that yes, "fish" were plentiful, but Alden would have to come very close inshore to get them and "that it might not be altogether prudent for his men to approach too near."[17]

Alden and *South Carolina*'s crew wasted no time in going after "fish" and celebrated the Fourth of July by capturing six small schooners: *Shark*, *Venus*, *Ann Ryan*, *McCanfield*, *Louisa* and *Dart*. After providing his unwilling guests a large dinner in honor of the date, he sent them into Galveston under a flag of truce on *Venus*. He destroyed *McCanfield* and *Louisa* after judging those vessels worthless as prizes.

Alden seized a total of ten small sailing vessels—and ran another aground—between July 4 and July 7. His operations slowed a bit after that, but he continued to make captures, including a pair of schooners carrying lumber, *General T.J. Chambers* and *Tom Hicks*. The former he sent in for adjudication as a prize, while the latter he scuttled after transferring her fifteen thousand board feet of lumber to his own ship.[18]

These captures, most within sight of Galveston and the JOLOs' observation post atop Hendley Row, undoubtedly rankled many on the island and made them anxious to strike back. On the morning of August 3, as *Dart* sailed close inshore trying to get a good look at Confederate batteries along the beach, the guns at the South Battery opened fire on the schooner. The Confederates' aim was good, putting a pair of shot through *Dart*'s mainsail before the little schooner could withdraw out of range. Alden, who had watched the whole incident from *South Carolina*, later reported that he was puzzled "that people could be so insane as to initiate hostilities with us when their town was so completely at our mercy." After waiting several hours for an explanation or renunciation of the Confederate gunfire, Alden got *South Carolina* under way and stood in toward the batteries. Closing to within about a mile of the beach, the Federal gunboat exchanged a hot-but-brief fire with both the South Battery and another Confederate battery farther to the east, near the foot of Fifteenth Street. This time everyone's shooting seems to have been off because *South Carolina* was not hit, and some of the Yankee shells overshot their targets, including at least one that landed in the middle of town but did not explode. A large crowd of local residents had gathered along the shore after hearing gunfire earlier in the day, eager at the prospect of witnessing a naval battle.[19]

USS *South Carolina* shells Galveston, August 1861. *Leslie's* Famous Leaders and Battle Scenes of the Civil War, *1896.*

"The people—men, women and children—flocked to the beach and lined the sand hills, interested spectators, unconscious of their danger, until aroused by the bursting of a huge shell in close proximity, which blew a Portuguese [immigrant] to pieces, and severely wounded three others, when there was a hasty and indiscriminate flight for the city."[20]

That same evening, local consuls representing the United Kingdom, France, Spain, Russia, the Netherlands and assorted German principalities addressed an angry letter of protest to Alden, condemning his actions as "acts of inhumanity unrecognized in modern warfare, and meriting the condemnation of Christian and civilized nations." Alden forwarded the consuls' letter to the Navy Department without comment but replied to the consuls himself by explaining the sequence of events leading up to the fight and demanding to know what they would have done in his place. Civilian casualties were to be greatly regretted, Alden said, but he rejected the notion that they were the result of callousness or negligence on his part. "Good God, gentlemen, do you think such an act could have been deliberate or premeditated? Besides, I would ask, was it not the duty of the military commandant who, by his act in the morning [i.e., firing on *Dart*], had invited me to the contest, to see that such [civilians] were out of the way? Did he not have all day to prepare?"[21]

Nothing came of the consuls' protest, but USS *South Carolina*'s engagement of the shore batteries (and inadvertently, the city beyond) had a profound and immediate effect on the citizens of Galveston. "A general *hegira* set in," one chronicler wrote several years later:

Families and household goods were hastily moved to the interior; merchants closed their stores, and removed their goods to Houston and other points in the state; cotton factors and buyers quickly sought a more secure locality in which they could carry on their business; banks were closed, and their deposits removed. The exodus continued until the homes, business houses and streets presented a dreary and desolate appearance...Grim, horrible war was at the threshold of the city, and laid his paralyzing hand upon its trade, its commerce, and its industries. A pall had fallen on its busy, bustling thoroughfares, that was to hang over them like a cloud for four long, weary and devastating years.[22]

The war had come to Texas.

Chapter 3

UNDER SAIL

To the Confederates that produce the cotton;
to the Yankees that maintain the blockade and keep up the price of cotton;
to the Britishers that buy the cotton and pay the high price for it.
Here is to all three, and a long continuance of the war,
and success to blockade runners.
—a blockade runner's toast, as recorded by William Watson

When USS *South Carolina* first took up station off Galveston in July 1861, nominally putting the entire Texas coast under the Federal blockade, Captain Alden snapped up several small sloops and schooners attempting to slip in or out of Galveston. Several of these he retained, including *Dart*, *Shark* and *Sam Houston*. Alden had these fitted with small guns and used them as tenders.

Although Alden and *South Carolina* would soon be transferred elsewhere, while he was on the Texas coast he was energetic and tenacious in enforcing the blockade. In September, Alden's lookouts spotted a schooner approaching Galveston. Alden gave chase in *South Carolina*, accompanied by his tender *Sam Houston*. Alden quickly overhauled the little schooner, on whose transom was painted the name *Soledad Cos*, with a home port of Tampico, Mexico. Alden sent an officer to inspect the vessel's papers. The schooner's master, Bill Johnson, made a desperate effort to avoid being taken. He quickly shaved his cheeks very close, rubbed them with white powder to make himself look deathly pale and retired to his bunk in his darkened cabin. When the officer from *South Carolina* arrived and was told that *Soledad Cos*'s master was in his cabin, near death with yellow fever (see Chapter 5), the officer immediately returned to *South Carolina* to fetch the ship's surgeon. When that officer reached the schooner, he looked down into the cabin just long enough to see the "dying" man inside moaning and coughing before he, too, returned to the Federal warship and reported to Alden that he deemed it unsafe to put a prize crew aboard.

At this point, Alden was getting suspicious; he thought he recognized the schooner. He then went over to the schooner, opened the hatch to the master's cabin wide to admit more light and climbed down into the cabin to get a good look for himself. After a moment, Alden said quietly, "You've played this one out, Johnson, and you'd better get up." Johnson immediately admitted the ruse. Alden had indeed recognized the vessel as *Anna Taylor*; under Johnson, she had been one of the first vessels to come out from Galveston to carry messages from Alden when he had arrived on station two months before. Johnson had taken his centerboard schooner, which drew only about three feet with the centerboard up, out through San Luis Pass at the western end of Galveston Island; sailed her to Tampico, where he arranged for a "sham sale" of the vessel; had her registered as a (neutral) Mexican schooner; and then continued on to Vera Cruz for a cargo. The twenty tons of coffee Johnson was bringing back would have fetched him a tidy sum in Galveston or Houston, even early in the war. In the actual event, it netted $3,223.85 at a prize court auction in New York, all of which went to the U.S. Treasury and the men involved in the *Soledad Cos*'s capture.[23]

Bill Johnson's ability to take *Anna Taylor* out of Galveston by way of the very shallow West Galveston Bay and San Luis Pass illustrates the one great advantage that small sailing vessels had over larger steamships: the ability to get in and out of the myriad small bays and inlets that make up much of the Gulf Coast. Although their cargo capacity was very limited—usually under one hundred bales of cotton outbound or perhaps twenty-five tons of other cargo—they were inexpensive to purchase and provide crews for. A sloop or schooner could, if necessary, lower all of its sails and spars to the deck, making it nearly invisible at a distance, and sailing vessels didn't leave a telltale smudge of coal smoke on the horizon when under way. The sailing vessel's great disadvantage, of course, was that it was subject to the vagaries of weather. A schooner might outrun a steam blockader for a while in ideal conditions, but it could rarely escape a long chase as the wind shifted during the day. A sloop caught in a dead calm was doomed.

A becalmed blockade-running schooner is chased by rowed launches from a Federal warship. *Illustration by Captain Byng, from William Watson's* The Adventures of a Blockade Runner, *1892.*

Over time, as more Union vessels became available for blockade duty, the U.S. Navy became increasingly successful in capturing or destroying sailing runners. Sometimes the blockaders acted with considerable boldness. For example, a little after noon on April 5, 1862, lookouts aboard the screw steamer USS *Montgomery* spotted a large schooner anchored inside San Luis Pass. *Montgomery's* commander, Lieutenant Charles Hunter, decided on a ruse and hoisted a British ensign at the peak and a Confederate flag at his foremast, making as if he wanted to communicate with the Confederate battery on shore. In due course, a boat from the nearby fort set out for the "British" ship anchored off the bar; Hunter had the nine men aboard quickly hustled down below as prisoners. Around sunset, he sent the captured boat, along with *Montgomery's* whaleboat, across the bar with orders to capture or destroy the schooner. The boats tried to get in past the Confederate battery in the darkness without being seen, but they were spotted, and the troops on shore opened fire. None of the Union sailors was hit, and now they began pulling hard at the oars to get alongside the schooner. They succeeded in taking the schooner's seven-man crew completely by surprise, despite the gunfire from the fort. The schooner turned out to be *Columbia*, of Galveston, loaded with cotton and ready to sail for Jamaica. As the Union sailors were preparing to get *Columbia* under way, a sloop appeared out of the darkness and came alongside. In it were *Columbia*'s master and seven passengers from Galveston, who intended to sail in her to Jamaica. These, too, became prisoners.

The officer in charge of the expedition, Acting Master Thomas Pickering, now had to deal with other problems. Both tide and wind were streaming against them, making it difficult or impossible to get the big schooner safely past the Confederate battery. Pickering ordered his men to set fire to *Columbia* and, with the sloop in tow, began pulling hard for the channel in their boats. They exchanged shots with the fort but succeeded in getting past it without injury. Pickering had his little flotilla anchor just inside the breakers on the San Luis Pass bar to await daylight. At dawn, the surf was still roiling, so Pickering, fearing the loss of the sloop in rough water with all on board, released the sloop and his prisoners to return to the safety of the bay. Pickering and the other two boats made it safely back to USS *Montgomery*. In exchange for the loss of one crewman seriously injured by the accidental discharge of another sailor's carbine, Pickering had destroyed a large schooner and her cargo of cotton that, by daylight, was seen to be "burned to the water's edge."[24]

While steam blockade runners would rely largely on speed and stealth for their success, the men who tested the blockade under sail seem to have been more inventive and clever about it; perhaps they had to be. Like Bill Johnson, feigning yellow fever in his cabin aboard *Soledad Cos*, the masters of sailing runners resorted to a number of attempts at brazen deception. A good example of the tricks used by both sides can be found in the story of the capture of the large British-flagged schooner *Water Witch* at Aransas Pass in August 1862. The sailing bark USS *Arthur* was anchored inside the pass, guarding the approaches to Corpus Christi. When a strange sail was sighted offshore on the evening of August 23, *Arthur*'s commanding officer, Lieutenant J.W. Kittredge, sent two men ashore on St. Joseph's Island, on the north side of the pass. These men displayed two lanterns on the beach, which Kittredge knew to be the signal to runners that the entrance channel was not blockaded. The following morning, the schooner began standing in over the breakers, into the pass. When the schooner's master became suspicious and tried to put about, Kittredge fired a shot across her bow, and the schooner hove to, running up the British Red Ensign. The master claimed his vessel to be *Water Witch*, of Kingston, Jamaica, and presented papers stating that she carried "general cargo, salt, shoes, drugs, rope, etc." bound for Matamoros. The schooner's master insisted he had been blown off course, but Kittredge noted that the schooner had lay at anchor off the channel at Aransas all evening, displaying the signal for a pilot to come out and guide him inside. Upon further examination, the vessel proved to have been "whitewashed," transferred to a foreign, neutral registration to hide her original identity. In fact, the big schooner was the former *Jo Sierra* of Galveston, which had run out of that port several months before with three hundred bales of cotton. Now, with a new name and new flag, her master, Thomas B. King, was attempting to run her back into a Confederate port with munitions. When Kittredge's men opened the schooner's hold, beneath a tier of salt kegs they found 150 twenty-five-pound kegs of fine-grained English gunpowder, milled for use in rifles. Kittredge estimated the value of both ship and cargo at $10,000.[25]

False signals, hidden cargoes, neutral flags and forged sailing papers were all part of the complex game played by blockade runners and the naval personnel who set out to catch them. One of the most successful runners under sail was William Watson, a Scotsman born on the Clyde in 1826. Watson emigrated to the Caribbean in 1845 and by the beginning of the war was living in Baton Rouge, Louisiana, where he was part owner in a sawmill and a steamboat business. Watson enlisted in the Confederate army after the bombardment of Fort Sumter. After a year's service with the Third Louisiana Infantry, Watson sought and received a discharge in July 1862 after his original term of enlistment ended. He was still a British subject and thus was not subject to compulsory reenlistment as outlined in the First Confederate Conscription Act of 1862.[26]

Watson's home in Baton Rouge was by then under Federal occupation, so Watson was forced to make a new living. He acquired a small, two-masted centerboard schooner, seventy-eight feet long, that he named *Rob Roy*. The schooner was perfectly suited to blockade running on a small scale, drawing about four feet, nine inches with the centerboard up and thirteen feet with the board down. The schooner was nearly flat-bottomed. Vessels like Watson's were not well adapted to riding out heavy seas, but they had other advantages. "These vessels," Watson wrote, "are peculiarly adapted for crossing the shallow bars which block the entrances to many of the inland bays and rivers on the coasts of the Southern States and Mexico, and also for the shoals and reefs of the Bahamas; and it is there that they are thoroughly understood, built, and navigated to perfection."[27]

Watson's first order of business was to "whitewash" the schooner in Belize, Honduras, then newly established as a British colony. In his memoir, *The*

Watson's centerboard schooner *Rob Roy*. *Illustration by Captain Byng, from* The Adventures of a Blockade Runner, *1892.*

Adventures of a Blockade Runner, Watson described the bureaucratic sleight-of-hand involved. He also noted that it was not only would-be blockade runners that engaged in the practice but also plenty of Yankee merchants, fearful that a Confederate raider like *Alabama* might take their vessel if they were caught sailing under the Stars and Stripes:

> *To effect this the usual way was to procure a British subject to assume the ownership, or stand godfather, as it was called, and a bill of sale was made out transferring the vessel to him, and if the transfer was made within the United States, the British Consul granted a provisional register to take the vessel to a British port.*
>
> *The British subject, or godfather, granted back to the real American owner letters or power of attorney to do what he pleased with the vessel, so that it often happened that some British subject—often a clerk or lad in a shipping-office—was nominal owner of several vessels...[As] a provisional register holds good for only six months, it was necessary to send the vessel at once to a British port, to be entered upon the British shipping-list, and obtain a permanent register and official number.*
>
> *The vessel was generally loaded with American goods, and dispatched to some British port, where the goods were sold cheap for specie, and the vessel put under a permanent register, and that port then became the hailing port*

of the vessel. This was the cause of the West India market being at that time glutted with American goods.[28]

Watson and *Rob Roy* eventually made three round voyages running the blockade into Texas—two to Galveston and one to the Brazos River. His exhaustively detailed memoir, reprinted by the Texas A&M Press in 2001, is rightly considered a classic among blockade-running memoirs and the only one that deals almost exclusively with operations under sail in the Gulf of Mexico.[29]

The Brazos River and the settlement at Velasco were a destination for many small sailing runners. The bar at the mouth of the river was treacherous, but once across, vessels were well protected. Small craft could be towed up to the river port of Columbia (now East Columbia), the terminus of the Houston Tap and Brazoria Railroad. By that route, through Houston, the lower reaches of the Brazos connected to the more densely settled eastern parts of the state, making the shipment of cotton and other cargoes almost as easy as at Galveston. The mouth of the Brazos River was narrow, as well, guarded by fortifications on both sides, so a Union cutting-out expedition like Pickering's at San Luis Pass would be extremely hazardous to attempt.

A lack of available ships prevented the U.S. Navy from maintaining an around-the-clock watch off the Brazos until the latter part of 1863, but attempts to get in and out of Velasco continued right through the end of the war. One of the more remarkable incidents there occurred in May 1864, when USS *Kineo* stopped and seized the schooner *Sting Ray*, nominally of British registry, some miles off the mouth of the river. *Kineo*'s commander, Lieutenant Commander John Watters, was suspicious of the schooner's paperwork, which claimed she was sailing from Havana to Matamoros. Not wanting to delay *Kineo*'s return to the river mouth, Watters put a boarding party on board the schooner, under the command of Acting Ensign Paul Borner, with instructions to follow *Kineo* back to her station.

Sting Ray's crew, however, had other plans. While Borner was busy poking around in the schooner's cabin, looking for incriminating documents, the schooner's master, Dave McClusky, invited the enlisted Union sailors down into the hold to sample some of the liquor on board. The sailors, whose taste for alcohol exceeded their own good sense, complied and were soon so inebriated that two "lay helplessly on deck and the rest were so drunk that they did not know what they were about."[30]

Blockade-running schooner caught in a gale. *Illustration by Captain Byng, from* The Adventures of a Blockade Runner, *1892.*

Borner and another seaman who challenged McClusky and his crew were quickly overpowered and disarmed. One of the stuporous Union sailors, startled at the commotion around him, tried to get to his feet, lost his balance and fell overboard; McClusky tossed a wooden spar after him to use as a lifesaver. Another Union bluejacket, left in the ship's boat tied astern as a boat keeper, was cut adrift as *Sting Ray* raced for the shore. Lieutenant Commander Watters pursued them in *Kineo* until the water became too shallow to continue and watched helplessly as McClusky ran his schooner gently up onto the beach, where they were soon joined by a troop of Confederate cavalry. *Kineo* doubled back to pick up the sailor who went overboard from *Sting Ray*. The man who had fallen into the water was, despite his long immersion, still "in a beastly state of intoxication, crazy drunk and howling" when his comrades fished him out.[31]

Blockade running under sail in Texas, and the Gulf of Mexico in general, contributed a great deal to the aggregate total of cotton, supplies and people trading between the Confederacy and neutral ports in Cuba, Honduras, Jamaica and Mexico. Marcus Price, in his exhaustive tabulations of blockade running during the war, calculated that sailing ships or those of "unascertained type" attempted more than 2,200 one-way trips through the Federal blockade in the Gulf of Mexico. On the whole, they were extraordinarily successful, getting through the Union cordon more than 80 percent of the time over the four years of war. Despite the real disadvantages of relying on the wind, it was only in the latter part of the war that their success rate dropped dramatically below that of steam-powered runners.[32] By grit and sheer numbers, they accomplished a very great deal, a few dozen tons at a time.

Chapter 4

COASTAL DEFENSE AND THE ESCAPE OF *LAVINIA*

It can not but be looked upon as a miserable business when six good steamers, professing to blockade a harbor, suffer four vessels to run out in one night.
—*Secretary of the Navy Gideon Welles*

The bombardment of Galveston's shore batteries (and the city beyond) by USS *South Carolina* in August 1861 convinced both residents and military officials on the Texas coast that the Federal blockade was in earnest. Overall commander of the new Confederate District of Texas, New Mexico and Arizona was Paul Octave Hébert, a Louisiana native who had graduated at the top of his class at West Point in 1840 and later served as governor of his home state. Hébert was a capable organizer and took basic measures to set up a defense of Galveston and the upper coast. He reinforced and expanded the batteries along the Gulf of Mexico at Galveston and, lacking a naval force of any kind, arranged to charter a collection of civilian riverboats to transport men, munitions and supplies around the bays and bayous along the coast.[33]

Nevertheless, Hébert was not a forward-thinking officer, and he did not believe that Galveston—located on an island and connected to mainland Texas by a single, two-mile-long railroad trestle—could be adequately defended. He said as much in a memorandum to Confederate secretary of war Judah P. Benjamin in October 1861 arguing that "owing to the superior naval armaments of the enemy and his entire possession of the sea, it will be almost impossible to prevent a landing at some point upon this extensive and unprotected coast. I have settled upon it as a military necessity that he must be fought on shore or in the interior." Hébert went on to call for a defense force of some fifteen thousand men, of whom three to four thousand would be required for the defense of far south Texas near the Rio Grande and the border with Mexico.[34]

Hébert was not popular with his soldiers. An account published after the war—and undoubtedly informed by knowledge of his ultimate failure to defend Galveston—presents an unflattering picture of the man:

> He proved to be a man of no military force or practical genius, though a West Pointer, and had enjoyed the advantages of military associations in Europe, the reflex of which appeared rather to damage his usefulness than otherwise. He brought with him so much European red-tapeism, and being a constitutional ape, that he preferred red-top boots, and a greased rat-tail moustache, with a fine equipage, and a suite of waiters, to the use of good, practical common sense…Everybody became tired and disgusted with the General and his policy. He was too much of a military coxcomb to suit the ideas and ways of a pioneer country; besides, he was suspected of cowardice.[35]

Hébert was not a coward, but neither was he really invested in defending a part of the coast he deemed undefendable. When Union blockading forces off the coast grew in number and aggressiveness in the late summer of 1862, Hébert convinced himself that Galveston was already as good as lost and suspended all ongoing work on the batteries on the island in favor of reinforcing a large sand fort on the mainland, at the end of the railroad trestle stretching to Galveston. Hébert also had the largest guns removed from the island, except for a single piece covering the entrance to the harbor at Fort Point. Galvestonians complained bitterly that Hébert, an old artilleryman by military specialty, loved his precious guns more than he loved the city.[36]

So it was that when Union gunboats steamed into the Galveston entrance channel on October 4, 1862, there was virtually no defense offered. Most of the artillery positions around the island were filled with fake cannon—"Quakers," as they were known—rough-carved from wood and painted a shiny black to simulate the real thing. The largest serviceable gun on the island, a ten-inch piece at Fort Point, was quickly knocked off its mount by Federal gunfire, and two smaller guns were unable to reply effectively against the Union vessels. Hébert ordered his officers on the scene to stall for time, evacuate the city and spike the few remaining guns.

The senior Confederate officer on the island, Colonel Joseph Jarvis Cook, managed to negotiate with the Federals a four-day cease-fire to evacuate noncombatants; during that interval, he also managed to remove a large quantity of military stores and some of the artillery pieces that remained on the island. When U.S. Navy commander William Renshaw's little flotilla of converted ferryboats finally entered the harbor on October 8, they had captured the best harbor in the Confederacy west of Mobile.[37]

For his failure to mount any sort of real defense of the island, Hébert was promptly sacked and replaced by John Bankhead Magruder, a commander from the eastern theater. Magruder had acquired the not-entirely complimentary nickname of "Prince John" for both his love of amateur theatricals and his elegant sartorial style. Magruder was a capable commander but had run afoul of Robert E. Lee during the Seven Days Battles, when at Malvern Hill (July 1, 1862) a convoluted mix-up of orders resulted in a series of failed assaults against an impregnable Union line. Lee subsequently reorganized his army, and Magruder, having been relieved of command, soon found himself en route to Texas to see what could be made of the mess there.

Magruder's first order of business would be to retake Galveston. Even before he arrived at Houston, he was consulting with Confederate officers who were certain that the island could be recaptured. Unlike Hébert, Magruder had a gift for unconventional thinking. Over the next several weeks, Magruder formulated a plan for retaking Galveston, cobbling together a makeshift force of converted civilian river steamers, dismounted Confederate cavalry and artillery pieces removed from the island by Colonel Cook during the cease-fire. Magruder's plan was complex, requiring a simultaneous nighttime attack by infantry, artillery and gunboats on the Federal forces holding the harbor at Galveston. After several delays, Magruder's forces finally got underway on the afternoon of December 31, 1862, and launched their attack around 4:00 a.m. on New Year's Day 1863. The attack was almost a total success, resulting in the seizure of one intact Union gunboat, *Harriet Lane*; the complete destruction of another Federal warship, USS *Westfield*; and the capture of several companies of the Forty-second Massachusetts Infantry that had been encamped on one of the wharves. In addition, Magruder's attack briefly lifted the blockade of Galveston completely. The senior Union officer surviving the attack, Richard Law, failed to resume a blockading station off the entrance to Galveston Bay and instead led his entire force all the way back to the mouth of the Mississippi to report the calamity to his superiors. The assistant secretary of the navy, Gustavus Fox,

David Glasgow Farragut, commander of the West Gulf Blockading Squadron, 1862–64. *Library of Congress.*

wrote to Rear Admiral David Glasgow Farragut, commanding the Union's West Gulf Blockading Squadron, that "the Galveston disaster is the most melancholy affair ever recorded in the history of our gallant navy. Five naval vessels driven off by a couple of steam scows with one gun which burst at the third fire and the attack made by soldiers, our prestige is shaken." Farragut himself was both dismayed and infuriated at the Galveston debacle, believing that a tension, a nervousness, a "nightmare" had afflicted his officers. "All our disaster at Galveston has been caused by it," Farragut wrote.[38]

The loss of Galveston was a serious setback for Farragut, one of three his squadron would experience in January 1863 alone. (The other two were the sinking of the side-wheeler USS *Hatteras* by the Confederate raider *Alabama* on January 11 and the capture of the sailing ship USS *Morning Light* off Sabine Pass on January 21.) Farragut commanded the West Gulf Blockading Squadron for almost three years—from its creation in January 1862 until late November 1864—using his ships aggressively both to maintain the blockade and to take strategic Confederate points along the Gulf and the lower Mississippi. Although he was in his early sixties, Farragut went about his duties with the vigor of a much younger man; for years he did a handspring annually on his birthday just to show that he could. He was also, perhaps, a little vain about his appearance. An officer who served under him later wrote that "in his later years he was partially bald...which he to some extent concealed by the arrangement of the hair." The admiral sported a comb-over.[39]

The officer Farragut sent to reinstate the blockade off Galveston, Commodore Henry H. Bell, discovered upon his arrival that work was already underway to reinforce the city's defenses. Having gambled on a risky plan to recapture the city, General Magruder had no intention of losing it again. He set about turning the island into an armed camp, and the engineering officers who had helped plan the recapture of Galveston were put to work building miles of earthworks and forts, some of which were connected by rail to enable the rapid transfer of guns and munitions. Piles were driven in lines across the harbor to prevent Union warships from entering unmolested as they had in October 1862, and mines were placed as well. In March, Commodore Bell reported observing two hundred or three hundred men working on the narrow strip of land connecting the battery at Fort Point to the city. Bell correctly guessed that the men were grading a route for a rail line. He decided not to fire on them, as "having shelled working parties before on this neck of land without materially interrupting their work, I considered it impotent and a waste of ammunition."[40]

The men Bell saw were almost certainly African American slaves, who comprised almost all of the labor force under Magruder's command. A formal report by one of Magruder's engineers, Colonel Valery Sulakowski, written on the last day of April 1863 gives the total number of laborers as 601, of whom 481 were assigned to labor gangs, 42 were employed as cooks and 78 were sick in the hospital. Sulakowski reported that of the 481 at work, "40 are at the saw-mills, 100 cutting and carrying sod (as all the works are of sand, consequently the sodding must be done all over the works), 40 carrying timber and iron, which leaves 301 on the works, including [harbor] obstructions." He went on to project that a force of 1,000 slave laborers would be required to complete the defensive works in three weeks, noting that it would take eight weeks at current levels. "The work of [white] soldiers amounts to very little," Sulakowski noted, "as the officers seem to have no control whatever over their men. The number of soldiers at work is about 100 men, whose work amount to 10 negroes' [sic] work."[41]

A visiting British officer, Arthur Fremantle, wrote that the slaves he saw had been "lent by the neighboring planters," but this elides the difficulty officers like Sulakowski had in securing laborers in the first place. The reality is that the officers charged with preparing the defense of Galveston and the Texas coast were always struggling to obtain the labor they needed and often came up short. This was a common pattern across the South during the war as large slaveholders were reluctant to turn over their work force (and primary financial asset) to the military, regardless of the terms offered. In the spring of 1862, the *Houston Telegraph* published an order of General W.R. Scurry calling on planters in southeast Texas to provide men to set up fortifications on the island. Scurry called for planters to send one-fourth of the male slave population so that "the Island can be made impregnable, and the State saved from the poluting [sic] tread of armed abolitionists." Scurry assured planters that good quarters, provisions and medical care would be provided and offered payment to the slaveholder of thirty dollars per month for each slave employed. Scurry also encouraged planters to send their slaves' regular overseers, offering them sixty dollars per month in compensation.[42]

After retaking Galveston on New Year's Day 1863, General Magruder took up the work of building up the defenses of the island with renewed energy. But like Scurry before him, Magruder also found that obtaining sufficient labor was a problem. When, immediately after the battle, Magruder called for area planters to provide one-half of their adult male slaves to work on building up fortifications, few responded. Magruder was eventually able to secure a large number of slaves to work on the island's defenses, but it remained a vexing problem. Gangs of impressed slaves continued to be used at Galveston through the end of the war, maintaining the entrenchments and providing general labor in support of the military garrison. As the situation throughout the state gradually deteriorated, the call was also made for yet more slave labor to keep the civilian infrastructure

A large "Second National" Confederate flag believed to have been flown at Galveston by Major Charles R. Benton, chief ordinance officer for the garrison there. Original image corrected for perspective by the author. *Texas State Library and Archives Commission.*

going. In October 1864, Magruder's successor, Major General John George Walker, would call on planters to volunteer their slaves "for a few weeks" to work on repairing railroads. Though Walker appealed to the planters' "sense of duty and patriotism," he openly threatened general impressment if sufficient numbers of slave laborers were not provided. Impressment, Walker warned, "seems unavoidable."[43]

Work on the batteries, entrenchments and connecting rail lines continued through the summer of 1863 until, on August 28, Confederate brigadier general Henry McCullough announced that, having now made sufficient progress surrounding the city with batteries and other field works, "the city of Galveston and vicinity are entrenched camps" henceforth subject to military regulation and discipline.[44]

One of the challenges Magruder faced in the months following the recapture of Galveston was what to do with the former U.S. gunboat *Harriet Lane*. The side-wheel steamer had not been seriously damaged during the fight on New Year's Day 1863, so work began almost immediately on putting her into Confederate service in some capacity. It was at this point that the ship's status became very complicated.

The Confederate prize commissioner, in charge of assessing and distributing captured Union vessels and property, was Philip C. Tucker, a local attorney who also happened to be a major on General Magruder's staff. Acting as prize commissioner, Tucker appointed to the ship a master and other officers, who took charge of making necessary repairs. Magruder, who had little experience with maritime law but had a grand vision for converting the ship to a commerce raider along the lines of CSS *Florida* or CSS *Alabama*, put out a call for experienced seamen to prepare the steamer for a cruise against Yankee merchantmen. The prize commissioner protested, arguing that the ship was under control of the civil courts and that until they disposed of her, Magruder and the military had no jurisdiction. The commissioner also argued that since a formal adjudication of the ship and its transfer to the Confederate navy was lacking, a cruise such as the one proposed by Magruder might be viewed as piracy. Magruder, perhaps preoccupied with more pressing concerns, shelved his plans and allowed the ship's guns and munitions to be removed.[45]

Offshore, the Federal officers of the reestablished blockade off Galveston were deeply worried about *Harriet Lane* slipping out of the harbor. On several occasions, the Union warships attempted to bombard the captured ship at extreme long range, without causing serious damage to their target but dropping shells all around the city instead. Francis Davenport, the executive officer aboard USS *Sciota*, recalled one of these incidents in which his ship steamed up into the entrance channel and began methodically lobbing shells at the former Union gunboat. The Confederate battery at Fort Point returned fire at the extreme range of about two and half miles. Davenport found being under fire unnerving

> *on account of the time elapsing between the puff of smoke and the arrival of the shot; the time was probably only ten seconds, but if a fellow was dancing around you with a big club, and you were waiting for him to hit you most anywhere, you wasn't sure where, time would be time. A puff of white smoke would shoot out from the fort, and we knew that something was coming. After a while you would hear a murmuring sound, like the wind in a distant grove, growing deeper and fuller until, like the blast of a hurricane, it rushed over and struck the water nearby, throwing a column fifty feet into the air, simultaneously relieving the suspended respiration of 150 sets of lungs, whose owners were earning their living literally by the sweat of their brows.[46]*

The Union bombardment did little damage to the captured side-wheeler, instead dropping shells indiscriminately around the city. The decision was made to tow *Harriet Lane* up Galveston Bay, out of view of the blockading fleet, to complete whatever repairs would ultimately take place. Her spare water tanks, masts and other heavy equipment were removed to decrease her draft, and in early February, she was towed up the bay. The civil courts awarded possession of *Harriet Lane* to the Confederate navy in March 1863, but in the end, the U.S. Navy Department lost interest, thanks in part to a less-than-glowing report on the ship's prospects by a Confederate navy lieutenant sent to evaluate the prize. The Confederate navy kept *Lane*'s larger artillery pieces and had them shipped to Louisiana for use on another vessel. Two smaller guns were turned over to one of Magruder's engineers, Julius Kellersberger, for use in shore batteries. What remained of the former Union gunboat, the navy turned back to General Magruder.[47]

With few options left, Magruder and his staff began to think about running the former Union gunboat out through the blockade. If the ship could reach a neutral port like Havana, loaded with Confederate government-owned cotton, both the cargo and the ship herself could be sold to generate cash money for the purchase of supplies and materiel badly needed by Magruder's command.

In the end, Magruder did not use government-owned cotton and instead negotiated an arrangement with Houston merchant Thomas W. House (see Chapter 6). House, who was already heavily engaged in running cotton overland through the Mexican border at Matamoros, agreed to provide the cotton in return for a large share of the profit if and when the old *Lane* safely reached a neutral port. Preparations dragged on for months until, early in the spring of 1864, all was ready. Magruder had taken special precautions to keep his plans secret, assigning a purchasing agent to go on board the ship who was kept ignorant of the fact that the ship was owned by the Confederate government, in the event of her capture. Magruder also kept the Confederate government agent at Havana, Charles J. Helm, unaware of his plans, lest word leak there about the ship's anticipated arrival in Cuba.[48]

The Union blockaders off Galveston still had not forgotten about *Harriet Lane*, and they remained watchful for any attempt by the Confederates to run her out. Admiral Farragut, who had been so angered over the loss of the ship and the recapture of Galveston more than a year before, was fairly obsessed with retaking the old gunboat. Officers on the blockade picked up a steady stream of information from refugees and deserters who periodically escaped to the Union fleet offshore, describing preparations being made for the ship's attempt to escape. Some of the information was accurate, some not—but it all added up to increasing anticipation that something was coming soon.[49]

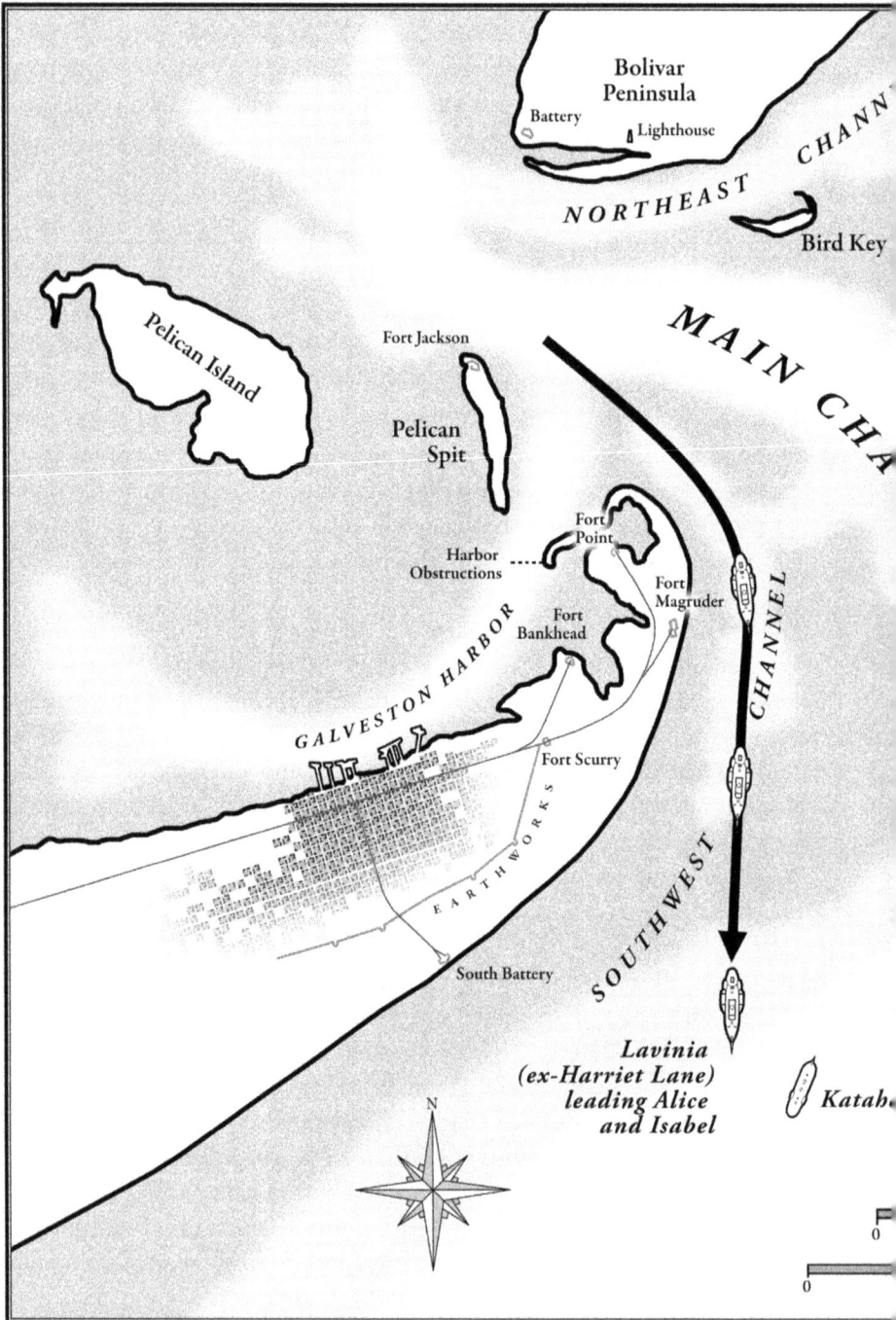

Bolivar
Peninsula

Battery   ▲ Lighthouse

CHANN

NORTHEAST   CHANNEL

Bird Key

MAIN CHA

Pelican Island

Fort Jackson

Pelican
Spit

Fort
Point

Harbor
Obstructions

Fort
Magruder

Fort
Bankhead

CHANNEL

GALVESTON HARBOR

Fort Scurry

MAIN CHA

E A R T H W O R K S

SOUTHWEST   CHANNEL

South Battery

N

Lavinia
(ex-Harriet Lane)
leading Alice
and Isabel

Katah

0

0

Owasco

Arizona

New London

Lackawana

Kineo

scape of the Runner

LAVINIA

April 30, 1864

1   2   3 Kilometers

2   3 Statute Miles

2   3 Nautical Miles

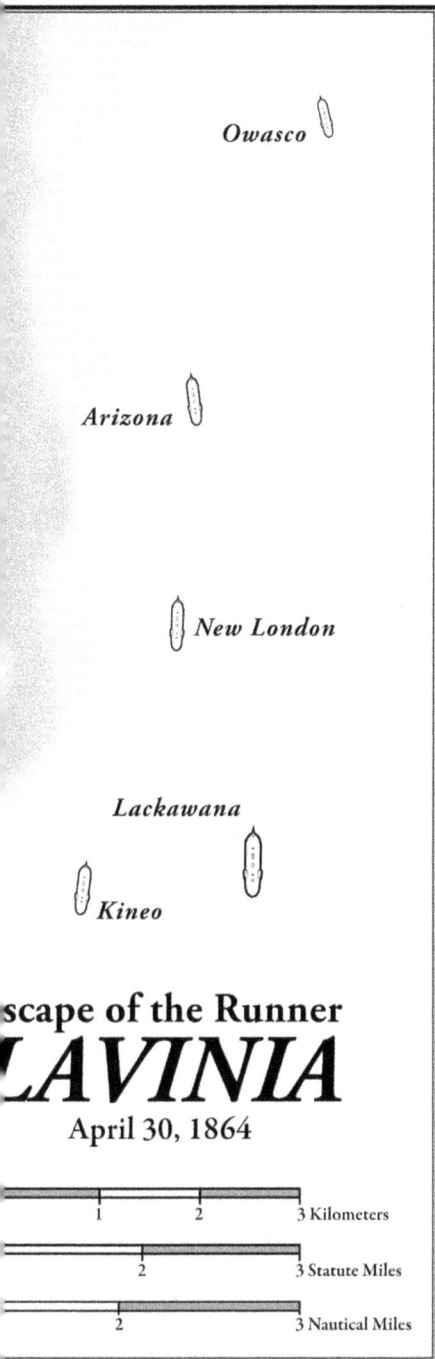

The Confederates made their breakout on the evening of April 30, a "dark, squally, and rainy" night on which the waning moon would not rise until nearly 4:00 a.m. *Harriet Lane*, now renamed *Lavinia* and under the command of Joseph C. Barnard, led the way out of the harbor, followed at fifteen-minute intervals by the steamers *Isabel* and *Alice*. The Union blockaders, aware of *Lavinia*'s deep draft, believed she would attempt her escape by the deeper, main channel and concentrated their forces there. The Confederates had encouraged this assumption in the days before the breakout, making a big show of placing buoys in the main channel as if anticipating the ships' exit by that route.[50]

But Magruder and his officers had fooled the blockaders; *Lavinia*, *Isabel* and *Alice* rounded the hook-shaped end of Galveston Island and ran out through the Southwest Channel, a narrower, shallower course that paralleled the shore. Only one Federal warship, *Katahdin*, was watching that route. At about 9:15 p.m., through intermittent rain squalls, *Katahdin*'s lookouts spotted *Lavinia* steaming by. However, mistaking her for another ship and believing his rockets would not be seen in any event due to the weather, *Katahdin*'s commander, John Irwin, did not fire off the prearranged signals to notify the other blockaders that a vessel was running out of Galveston.

The escape of *Lavinia*, *Alice* and *Isabel* from Galveston, April 30, 1864. *Original map by the author.*

Thinking he was chasing some other runner, he slipped his anchor cable and set out alone after the mysterious side-wheeler. Irwin continued after the mysterious ship in the darkness, briefly catching sight of her and then losing her again until daylight, when he recognized her as the old *Harriet Lane*. He also spotted a second runner, *Alice*, and spent the next several hours maneuvering to chase them down. Irwin lost sight of *Lavinia* at about 2:00 p.m. on May 1 and *Alice* at about 8:00 p.m.—almost twenty-four hours after the chase began. Desperate to keep up a full head of steam, *Katahdin*'s engineers shoveled not only coal into her furnaces but also firewood from the galley, lumber from the carpenter's stores, tar and even pork. Irwin, using both sails and steam power, continued to follow the runners' presumed track at full speed until broad daylight the following morning but found no further sign of the ships. Almost thirty-six hours after it began, the chase was over. With just fifteen tons of coal remaining in *Katahdin*'s bunkers, barely enough to return to her station off Galveston, Irwin reluctantly came about and set a course back to the Texas coast.[51]

If Irwin expected praise for his dogged pursuit of *Lavinia*, he would be disappointed. Farragut was livid, and he let Irwin know *exactly* who he held responsible: "I attribute the escape of those vessels to your not firing a gun and burning lights to give notice to the squadron of their running out. That you were afraid it would draw Captain Marchand from his station was not a proper reason for so great a dereliction of duty, as he was the proper person to judge of the propriety of leaving the channel unguarded and not you."[52]

Lavinia, *Alice* and *Isabel* arrived safely in Havana a week after running out by the Southwest Channel at Galveston, bringing with them an aggregate of about 1,750 bales of cotton. In June, Confederate secretary of war James Seddon wrote to General E. Kirby Smith, commanding the Trans-Mississippi Department, that the Confederate government agent in Havana, Charles J. Helm, had procured ten thousand rifles for the use of Confederate troops in the theater, adding that Helm would be putting these aboard inbound blockade runners "from time to time as opportunity offered." Seddon mentioned the arrival of both *Lavinia* and *Alice*, describing their cotton cargoes as being "exclusively on private account," but his subtext was clearly that the proceeds from them would go to paying for the munitions already contracted for. Seddon also reminded Smith of the recent change in Confederate law requiring that all vessels calling at Confederate ports devote half their cargo to government consignments, both inbound and out.[53]

Both *Alice* and *Isabel* returned to blockade running, but *Lavinia* remained bottled up at Havana for the remaining year of the war, the subject of much speculation and diplomatic wrangling between the United States and the Spanish governor general of Cuba. In January 1865, the ship was damaged—though not destroyed, as widely reported at the time—by a fire allegedly set by a disgruntled crew member who had not been paid. When the U.S. Navy finally retook possession of the paddle steamer after the war, the old ship and her worn-out engines were of little use to a service that already had a surplus of warships, so *Lavinia* (ex-*Harriet Lane*) was sold at auction. Her new owners removed her machinery, re-rigged her as a bark and, under the name *Eliot Richie*, put her into service between East Coast ports, Latin America and the Mediterranean. By the time the old gunboat, once a gem of the Union navy, foundered off the coast of Brazil in 1881, most people had long since forgotten *Harriet Lane*.[54]

But the old Yankee prize from the battle of January 1, 1863, was never forgotten in Galveston. As *Eliot Richie*, she called at Galveston on at least three occasions, the first time in the fall of 1872, bringing ice from Boston and taking on a load of cotton bound for Trieste.[55] Despite her now-mundane trade, an anonymous writer for the *Galveston Daily News* could not help but recall, in the turgid prose of the day, the old ship's past glories:

> *Mankind instinctively look with interest at the locality of great events, be it a battlefield, where every elevation tells the story of carnage and sacrifice; or the deck of a ship, where every nut and nail holds fast a reminiscence. The* Harriet Lane *will always be an object of interest to our people… discharging at Kuhn's Wharf the products of peaceful industry, instead of broadsides of shot and shell.*[56]

Chapter 5

ON THE BLOCKADE

[The blockade has] *gathered itself in a circle around the doomed rabbit of secession, and if the rabbit swells he's a goner.*
—Orpheus C. Kerr, 1862

The U.S. Navy was poorly equipped to mount a naval blockade of Confederate ports in the spring of 1861, even though the blockade was a key element in the Union's grand strategy. Like the South American constrictor for which it was named, the Anaconda Plan would, Lincoln and his advisors hoped, gradually squeeze the life out of the rebellion.

But establishing a blockade of the South was a job far easier said than done. Through April and May 1861, as planning for the blockade got underway in earnest, the Navy Department began flooding the offices of the U.S. Coast Survey with requests for charts of the southern states. The superintendent of the Coast Survey, Alexander Dallas Bache, urged Secretary of the Navy Gideon Welles to appoint a formal board to advise the navy on organizing the blockade. Welles agreed, giving Bache the authority to name other members as he desired. The committee would be known as the Blockade Strategy Board.[57]

Although the board was headed by a senior naval officer, Samuel F. DuPont, Bache was undoubtedly its guide. Under Bache's direction, the Coast Survey had meticulously recorded the bays, inlets and hydrographic features of the entire Gulf of Mexico. The charts compiled during Bache's long tenure as superintendent (1843–61) were the first comprehensive and scientific effort to chart the coast of Texas. Nonetheless, Bache and his

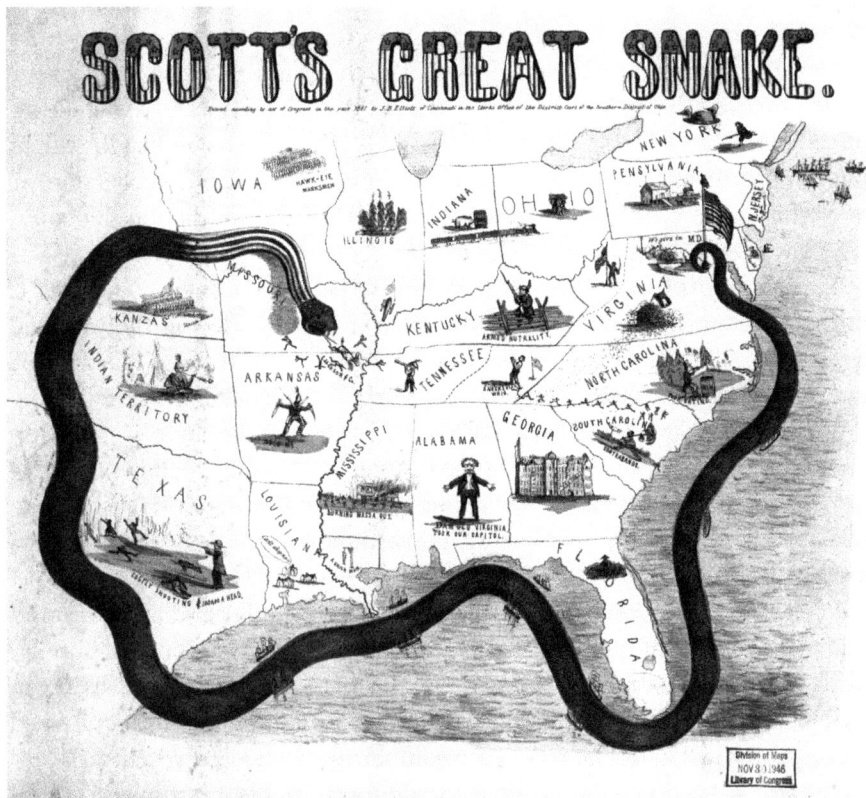

A contemporary cartoon mocking the Anaconda Plan as Winfield Scott's "Great Snake."
Library of Congress.

fellow board members woefully underestimated the resources necessary to blockade the Texas coastline effectively. Writing of the area from Grande Pass, Vermilion Bay, Louisiana, to the Rio Grande on the border with Mexico, a distance of about 425 nautical miles, Bache and the board suggested that "three or four efficient Vessels, which can take care of themselves at sea against storms and enemies, are required for the blockade of this portion of the coast."[58] One should be of light draft, they added, to patrol the numerous bays and inlets along the shore. It proved to be a grossly inadequate calculation; by the end of the war, a dozen Yankee blockaders anchored off the entrance to Galveston Bay would be a common sight.

The answer to the Union's desperate need for ships was much the same as it was for the Confederacy—to press into service anything that would float.

Navy Department agents fanned out in New York, Philadelphia, Boston and other ports, buying up civilian ships idled by the conflict and, in many cases, purchasing vessels still under construction. Although the U.S. Navy would go on to build many successful classes of warships during the conflict, including the famous turreted monitors, it was this rapidly assembled collection of makeshift naval vessels that carried the weight of the conflict on the coast, bays and rivers of the South.

Yankee sailors were different in several respects from their counterparts in the Union army. More than half of naval recruits during the war had worked in skilled trades in civilian life, as opposed to a large majority of men enlisting in the army who were categorized as farm laborers or working in unskilled trades. A full one-third of navy recruits, though, were either unemployed or listed no occupation in their enlistment documents; these were likely men from cities who had no regular employment but picked up odd jobs as they could. Not surprisingly, three-quarters of Union sailors came from Atlantic seaboard states.[59]

While immigrants made up about a quarter of the Federal army, around 45 percent of naval enlistees were foreign-born. (Overall, those of foreign birth represented about 27 percent of the men of military age living in Union states.) While many of these were longtime residents or naturalized citizens of the United States, a substantial number were recent arrivals. There are good reasons why more foreign-born men were drawn to naval service as opposed to the infantry or artillery. Army units—largely organized by individual states and drawing on companies and regiments formed in specific towns and counties—often had a strong "nativist sentiment" that discouraged foreign-born men from enlisting, except in units like the famed Irish Brigade. Both the U.S. Navy and the civilian maritime trades, by contrast, had a long tradition of multinational crews, offering a better chance for foreigners to assimilate into the service.[60]

African Americans made up a substantial part of the enlisted ranks of the Union navy. Their exact numbers are a matter of dispute, although a widely adopted figure of eighteen thousand wartime recruits would put them at more than 15 to 20 percent of the total, a substantially higher proportion than black soldiers in the Union army. African Americans had been present in the U.S. Navy before the conflict, representing about 2.5 percent of enlisted sailors before the war, when the navy maintained a quota dating back to 1839 that no more than 5 percent of monthly recruits could be men of color. That quota was waived during the exigency of the Civil War, opening naval service to a much wider pool of recruits. The proportion of

A sketch of Union ships on the blockade off Galveston in October 1864. The key to identifying the ships has been lost, but the vessel at top left is probably the division flagship, USS *Ossipee. Rosenberg Library*.

USS *Hatteras* was typical of the large civilian steamers purchased into the U.S. Navy for use on the blockade. She took two prizes off Sabine Pass before being sunk by the Confederate raider *Alabama* in January 1863. *Author's illustration.*

African American sailors on a typical U.S. Navy warship varied considerably over the course of the war and by location; the numbers of enlisted African Americans carried aboard ships' muster books peaked in 1863–64, at about 23 percent of the total. In the second quarter of 1864, just before the closing of Mobile as a blockade-running port and a corresponding boost in blockade running into Galveston, African Americans represented about 20 percent of the enlisted crews of the West Gulf Blockading Squadron, the division of the navy tasked with guarding both those ports.[61]

The presence of large numbers of African Americans in the U.S. Navy, though, should not be construed as an indicator of full integration or equality within the maritime service. Black sailors were routinely relegated to the most menial, dirtiest jobs on board or were assigned as officers' stewards. Relatively few rose above the rating of landsman, and they were frequently the butt of harassment and verbal abuse by white sailors. One or another form of segregation between white and black sailors was common, both in living arrangements and in work details. Racial barriers seem to have been most rigidly enforced aboard Union gunboats on the Mississippi, while on the blockade, a sort of "soft social segregation" among messes and off-watch activities seems to have been more common.[62] Such de facto arrangements are suggested in contemporary photographs of Union navy crews, where African American sailors are often gathered in a group rather than dispersed among their white shipmates. Nevertheless, African American sailors formed a sizeable share of the navy's personnel force, enabling the Union to keep many more ships manned and on the blockade than it might have otherwise.

One aspect of blockade duty that comes up often in Union sailors' accounts is the stupefying boredom that often set in. Unlike vessels in port, where liberty ashore was available, or at sea, where sailing the ship required around-the-clock attention, ships on the blockade moved relatively little and spent much of their time sitting and watching. Alfred Thayer Mahan, who would later achieve fame as a maritime historian and naval theorist, was a midshipman during the Civil War and served two tours aboard ships on the Texas coast in 1863 and 1864, off the relatively quiet location of Sabine Pass. Years later, he recalled that the dull routine wore the crews down mentally, if not physically:

> *Blockading was desperately tedious work, make the best one could of it. The largest reservoir of anecdotes was sure to run dry; the deepest vein of original humor to be worked out. I remember hearing of two notorious tellers of stories being pitted against each other, for an evening's amusement, when one was driven as a last resource to recounting that "Mary had a little lamb." [I] have never seen a body of intelligent men reduced so nearly to imbecility as my shipmates then were.*[63]

One thing that alleviated boredom was the opportunity to visit other blockading ships. During daylight hours and clear weather at Galveston, blockading ships would leave their night stations and anchor near the squadron flagship, which made passing communications easier, facilitated officers' conferences and gave off-duty officers a chance to visit friends on other ships. Such opportunity for socializing did not extend to enlisted crewmen, apart from those fortunate enough to be assigned as boats' crews, but it did serve as an opportunity for the men to pass along news and that staple of sailor life—scuttlebutt.[64]

One event that officers and enlisted men alike looked forward to was the arrival of the squadron's supply ship. These vessels typically appeared every two or three weeks, bringing with them provisions, mail, newspapers and magazines, parcels from home, munitions, spare parts for machinery, fresh hands and all the other things necessary to maintain an active blockade of a hostile shore. As soon as the supply ship anchored near the flagship, a dozen or more ships' boats would be pulling for her to retrieve their designated mail and provisions. Nonetheless, off Texas, neither the news nor provisions were very fresh. Mahan, who had previously served in the well-supplied blockade

USS *Sciota* off Galveston. *Illustration from Davenport,* On a Man-of-War.

fleet off South Carolina, recalled that off Charleston "supply vessels, which came periodically, and at not very long intervals, arrived with papers not very late, and with fresh provisions not very long slaughtered; but by the time they reached Galveston or Sabine Pass, which was our station, their news was stale, and we got the bottom tier of fresh beef."[65]

Sailors in the Union navy were generally a healthy lot, healthier on the whole than their counterparts in the army. This was due in large part to the fact that the navy was able to draw on long-established experience in keeping men healthy at sea. Most of the hundreds of naval officers appointed during the war came from the merchant service and thus had a solid background in shipboard management. The same was not true of the army, which had no counterpart in the civilian world and called upon the leadership of newly commissioned officers drawn from every professional background imaginable. Both afloat and ashore, more men died of disease than from combat, but about one in twelve Union soldiers would die of illness during the war, compared to about one in fifty Union sailors.[66]

One important factor in the relatively good health of the navy, as opposed to the army, was the relative abundance of clean, fresh water, at least on steamships. Steam from the ship's boilers could be routed to on-board distilling equipment. This ready availability of distilled water eliminated many of the waterborne diseases and parasites that plagued soldiers on shore, who generally had to draw their water from whatever local stream or well was available. Diseases like typhoid, parasitic worms, diarrhea and dysentery were all much less prevalent aboard ship than they were on shore.[67]

Nevertheless, the navy found itself in a constant struggle against sickness because even nonfatal illness reduced the effectiveness of the crew and the vessel. Remarkably, scurvy remained an ongoing problem for the navy, particularly among the blockading squadrons. Scurvy is a nutritional disease caused by a lack of vitamin C, which is commonly found in fresh vegetables and fruit, particularly citrus. Scurvy causes a general debilitating weakness, anemia, skin hemorrhages and gum disease and can be fatal. Although mariners in the nineteenth century did not know the exact mechanism of scurvy, they had a good empirical knowledge of both its treatment and prevention. As a result, occasional cases of scurvy among the blockaders came about not through ignorance or carelessness but due to the extremely long and complex supply chain that made it difficult to keep the fleet stocked with fresh provisions. The problem was especially acute for those ships and men of the West Gulf Blockading Squadron, who stood at the end of a very long supply chain. Winfield Scott Schley, a naval officer who would later rise to fame during the Spanish-American War, recalled that during his time on the blockade off Mobile, scurvy "was only avoided by the occasional relief which came to them afterward from the steamers bringing supplies of fresh meats and vegetables in amounts about enough for two or three days. The diet for the rest of the month was composed mainly of salted meats, cheese, hard bread, bad butter, inferior coffee and positively bad tea. It is indeed a wonder that the efficiency of the personnel was maintained at all under such condition."[68] At one point in the summer of 1862, the problem of scurvy had become so serious that Farragut had to send three ships of his command to northern ports to recover. Scurvy in particular seems to have plagued ships whose distance from regular sources of supply was extreme. Over the next three years, there were regular reports of the disease from vessels off the Texas coast where, as Farragut noted, "the ships are in much need of [vegetables] to avoid scurvy." The Union sailing vessel *Midnight*, for example, spent nine months in 1862 on continuous blockade duty, most of it on the Texas coast. During that time, her officers and crew had fresh provisions for just twenty-four days. When she was eventually relieved on station and returned to the fleet anchorage at the mouth of the Mississippi, some forty men—more than half her crew—were on the sick list with scurvy, dysentery and diarrhea. Afflicted vessels on the Texas blockade at various times included *Brooklyn* and, on at least two separate occasions, the bark *William G. Anderson*.[69]

One of the most dreaded diseases aboard ship was yellow fever. There was no cure for it (there still isn't), and the way it was transmitted was not understood. Yellow fever is a mosquito-borne viral disease varying widely in severity, exhibiting everything from flu-like symptoms to severe hepatitis and hemorrhagic fever. The disease has a normal incubation period of three to six days, during which time there are no outward symptoms of the illness. After this incubation period, most victims enter what is now termed the "acute phase" of the disease, during which they experience fever, headache, muscle pain, nausea and vomiting. These symptoms usually subside after three or four days, and the patient recovers. In some cases, however, within twenty-four hours, the disease enters its "toxic phase," and the patient develops jaundice (from whose appearance yellow fever gets its name) and complains of abdominal pain with vomiting. Patients bleed from the mouth, nose, eyes and stomach. Kidney function drops off and sometimes fails altogether, resulting in a rapid rise in the levels of toxins in the body. About half the patients who enter the toxic phase of the disease die within ten to fourteen days, while others usually recover gradually.[70]

***

Just as the blockade runners would learn, through trial and error, the most effective tactics for running in and out of Confederate ports, the Union navy became increasingly effective at stopping them. The biggest challenge during the early part of the war, as noted earlier, was simply the lack of ships to maintain the blockade. As the U.S. Navy grew in size and experience, though, it gained the flexibility necessary to gradually tighten the Anaconda's stranglehold on the Confederacy.

More often than not, it was the blockade runner who held most of the advantage. The masters and pilots aboard runners could generally choose the timing and location of their attempts to get through the cordon of Federal warships off a port, arranging their runs to coincide with dark, moonless nights or times of poor visibility. Blockade runners often carried local mariners to act as pilots, men who knew the currents and quirks of underwater topography that the runner could use to its advantage. Runners trying to enter a Confederate port would try to time their arrival to meet projected tidal conditions, while officers of outbound runners would wait carefully for just the right conditions. In Galveston, that often meant a trip to the JOLO station atop Hendley's Row. There, at dusk and using the lookout's telescopes, the blockade runner's officers would make careful note

Hendley's Row in Galveston, 2012. *Author's photo.*

of the positions of Union ships off the bar and plan their own route to avoid the gunboats.

As darkness approached, the blockaders would up-anchor and move to their assigned night positions. These positions were changed periodically, according to the number of blockading vessels available, weather and sea conditions and other factors. Buoys would be placed on anchor cables so that the blockader could recover the anchor later if it became necessary to slip the cable quickly and set off in pursuit of a runner. Below deck, the engineers kept up sufficient boiler pressure to get the ship moving at a moment's notice. Above deck, all lights were extinguished and unnecessary noise kept to a minimum in hopes of hearing a runner's paddlewheels thrashing along, even if the ship itself were obscured by fog or haze.

To cover the gaps between ships on station, each ship sent out one or more boats to patrol, each manned by an officer, seamen and Marines. Although they carried small arms, these boats' primary purpose was to make the alarm if they spotted a runner going in or out. For this, they were equipped with colored rockets, flares and other pyrotechnics. Assignment to a picket boat was arguably the most dangerous duty on the blockade; apart from the usual hazards of being in a small, open boat, there was also the risk of being blown ashore on Confederate-held territory or getting run down by either a runner or a blockader in hot pursuit. Tom Taylor, an Englishman who served as a sort of business manager for a fleet of runners, witnessed a close call in the early morning hours of February 24, 1865, while running into Galveston aboard *Banshee (II)*:

> *We had been under weigh some time, when suddenly we discovered a launch close to us on the port bow filled with Northern blue-jackets and marines. "Full speed ahead," shouted* [Captain Jonathan W.] *Steele, and we were within an ace of running her down as we almost grazed her with our port paddle-wheel.* [Frank] *Hurst and I looked straight down into the boat, waving them a parting salute. The crew seemed only too thankful at their narrow escape to open fire, but they soon regained their senses and threw up rocket after rocket in our wake as a warning to the blockading fleet to be on the alert.*[71]

The blockaders got steadily better at their job, roughly keeping pace with the increasingly skillful runners they opposed. Their skills would be needed because as the war dragged on, Texas would become a more frequent destination for runners, particularly in the closing months of the war. Even after the Confederate cause was clearly and irretrievably lost, the struggle between the runners and blockaders would reach its peak off the Texas coast.

Chapter 6
ALL ON CREDIT

She was six hundred tons,
She was manned by Scotia's sons;
She was the skipper's pride,
She sail'd from bonny Clyde;
She was sound from top to bottom,
She was built to carry cotton,
And to run the blockade in the morning!
—anonymous broadside, The Poet's Box, *Glasgow, 1873*

During the first months of the war, when the Union blockade of Confederate ports was more notion than fact, practically every vessel attempting to run the blockade was successful. Marcus Price, the historian who tabulated blockade-running activities, calculated that 97 percent of all attempts to run in or out of a Gulf port through the end of 1861—and 99 percent of attempts by steamships—got away clean.[72]

However, as time went on, and the Union blockade became more effective, there was an increasing recognition that the most effective runners were mid-sized, shallow-draft steamers, particularly those propelled by paddlewheels. Very large transatlantic steamers were both impractical and unnecessary; the ideal type turned out to be a fast coastal steamer, designed from the keel up to make short, quick passages between ports no more than a few days apart. A number of successful blockade runners, including *Denbigh*, began their lives as steamers carrying passengers and cargo around the western coasts of England and Wales.

As the war stretched into its second and third years, an increasing number of purpose-built runners began testing the blockade. Many of these were modeled on the "Clyde steamer," a vessel type that was honed in a similar sort of trade, carrying passengers and mails coastwise in the United Kingdom and across the Irish Sea. The steel-hulled paddle steamer *Banshee (II)*, launched at Glasgow in 1864, is a good example of the type. Measuring 252.6 feet long by 31.7 feet in width (not including the paddlewheels on either side), she had a length-to-beam ratio of nearly eight to one. At the same time, *Banshee (II)* probably drew no more than nine feet, fully loaded, a depth that would allow her to slip in and out of shallow Confederate harbors with relative ease. The steel-hulled runner *Will o' the Wisp*, launched at Renfrew on the Clyde in 1863, was smaller but even more extreme in her proportions, measuring 209.5 feet long by 23.2 feet wide, with a length-to-beam ratio of nine to one. With their long hulls, blade-like bows and shallow draft, these purpose-built runners were shaped very much like enormous canoes. This type of steamer was so well adapted to the conditions of blockade running that by the end of the war, the Union navy had bought about twenty captured Clyde-built runners and put them in service on the blockade against their former comrades.[73]

These coastal steamers were somewhat fragile and not well suited to hard driving in heavy seas. As with a high-strung racehorse, it was possible to drive such ships to their own destruction, and several were lost in winter storms crossing the Atlantic. William Watson, the Scot who had run the blockade into Texas several times under sail, took the Clyde-built steamer *Jeanette* out of Galveston in the spring of 1865, bound for Tampico. He got clear of the blockading fleet at Galveston but was chased by a Union gunboat the next day in a heavy, running sea. A rifled shot from the warship went through *Jeanette's* funnel, a few feet above the boiler, and Watson ordered some of the deck cargo of cotton bales to be stacked around the boiler for protection. No sooner had the bales been placed than

> *the engineer came running up to say that the vessel was buckling amidship. I looked and saw her bending up at the bow and stern, as she pitched in the seas. The taking away of the cotton bales from the bow and stern to place round the boiler had lightened her too much at the bow and stern, and weighted her too heavily amidships, and this caused her to strain in running before a heavy sea. All hands were immediately set to roll out bales towards the bow and stern to stiffen the vessel, and this was rather difficult work in a heavy sea...I saw from this incident the great importance of having the weight properly distributed on such fragile vessels.*[74]

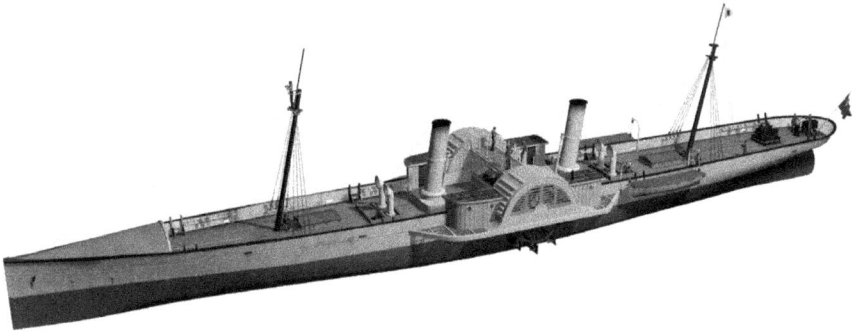

Digital reconstruction of the blockade runner *Will o' the Wisp. Author's illustration.*

Blockade runner *Denbigh* in heavy seas. *Author's illustration.*

The inherent brittleness of the ship's design was sometimes compounded by substandard construction, to the point of the workmanship being "grossly incompetent."[75] Tom Taylor, an Englishman who served as a sort of field operations officer for the Anglo-Confederate Trading Company, later recalled that "great things were expected" of the firm's new runner, *Will o' the Wisp*, when she first arrived at Nassau in the Bahamas. Taylor would soon discover, though, that she was "shamefully put together, and most fragile." She arrived leaking so badly that her master, Peter Capper, had to keep his engines running to power the pumps.[76] Soon after, on her first passage through the blockade into Wilmington, North Carolina, *Wisp* ran hard aground at full speed, further torquing her weakened hull. The ship's return voyage to Nassau proved to be a desperate sixty-hour struggle to stay afloat. "It was a very narrow escape," Taylor recalled, "[because] within twenty minutes after stopping her engines the vessel had sunk to the level of the water." Once again, the ship was patched up, but she proved to be "a constant source of delay and expenditure." Taylor eventually passed *Wisp* off onto some unsuspecting buyers "after having her cobbled up with plenty of putty and paint."[77] Despite her troublesome history, *Wisp* had nonetheless turned the Anglo-Confederate Trading Company a sizeable profit.

The quest for profit dominated affairs in Texas as well. There were fortunes to be made in blockade running, but as with most other enterprises, the main benefits accrued to those few who were well positioned to take advantage of it. Common citizens, who began the war with little capital and saw what they did have evaporate with the hyper-inflation of Confederate currency, struggled daily with the shortage of basic goods. By contrast, "General Magruder and his staff lived on the fat of the land. Several favored and adventurous merchants grew rich, honorably, by running the blockade. Dozens of army contractors got rich, any old way. The great mass of the real men were off at the front fighting for their country, and their families at home suffered for the absolute necessities of life. That is not a very nice picture, but it is a true one."[78]

It's probably more accurate to say that the "favored and adventurous merchants" grew rich*er* by running the blockade because they generally started out with the resources and business connections necessary to enter the trade. One of these was William Marsh Rice, a New Englander who came to Houston in 1838 and set up a general merchandise store with Ebenezer Nichols. The business prospered, and by 1860, Rice owned property, including slaves, amounting to $750,000.[79]

Rice was probably not a secessionist and likely saw the dissolution of the Union as a disaster. Nonetheless, he remained in Houston through the first years of the war, maintaining his business interests as best he could and contributing to various funds for the support of Confederate widows and military hospitals.[80] After the death of his wife Margaret in August 1863, though, he relocated first to Monterrey and then to Matamoros, Mexico, and continued trading in cotton and other supplies there. Because Mexico was neutral in the war, the little settlement of Bagdad, on the south side of the mouth of the Rio Grande, exploded during the war years with thousands of "peddlers, merchants, deserters, gamblers, swindlers, undercover agents, and whores from a dozen nations." Cotton moved out freely through Matamoros and Bagdad, and other material—such as munitions, medicines and consumer luxuries—came in to be shipped across the river to Brownsville and overland into the Texas interior. Everyone at Bagdad and Matamoros claimed a piece of the action, demanding usurious charges for lightering cargo, port fees, import duties and so on. Along with a flat 12.5 percent export duty charged on all outgoing cargoes by Mexican customs officials, the accumulated charges sometimes "far exceeded the value of the goods, and in many cases the owners...abandoned them altogether, leaving those who had made the charges to make the most of them."[81]

Rice thrived in this environment. He also recognized the inevitable defeat of the Confederacy, and in the spring of 1864, he instructed his son in Houston to sell off his company's entire inventory at auction for whatever it would bring in hard currency. As one of his biographers put it, Rice "had gone into the war a rich man [and] was one of those who came out of it even wealthier."[82]

The biggest speculator in blockade running into Texas was Houston merchant Thomas William House, an Englishman who emigrated to New York in his early twenties and soon made his way to Texas, where he took part in the revolution against Mexico in 1836. He opened a bakery in Houston in 1838 and quickly began building a mercantile empire through expansion into general wholesaling, moving vast quantities of merchandise through his warehouse. House's success enabled him to invest in other ventures that boosted commerce in the city. In 1851, he joined with Rice and two dozen other businessmen, merchants and river pilots to form a limited partnership known as the Houston and Galveston Navigation Company to operate a fleet of riverboats running between those two cities. The company quickly grew to carry the lion's share of the passenger and cargo trade between Houston and Galveston, with boats running daily in both directions.[83]

House was a strong supporter of the Confederate government of Texas, using his business connections and capital to trade in cotton and supplies for the rebellion. He donated money to soldiers' relief causes and supplies to local militia companies like the Houston Light Guard, which became known as the "Kid Glove Gentry" for the new gloves House supplied.[84] House became a trusted confidante of Confederate commanders in Texas, who relied on his connections and influence to facilitate activities that they, in their military roles, could not. General Magruder's reliance on House in outfitting the former Union gunboat *Harriet Lane*, refitted as *Lavinia*, to run the blockade to Havana has been noted in a preceding chapter. But House's

Thomas William House, the Houston merchant who dominated blockade running on the Texas coast. *Rosenberg Library*.

patriotic interests mostly paralleled those of his business, and he invested heavily in blockade running as part of his own mercantile enterprise. House maintained a residence in Galveston, and his young son Edward later recalled walking on the beach with his father late in the afternoon, making note of the Union gunboats offshore. If conditions were right, House would send instructions to the masters of his ships in port to attempt to slip out that night. If the same Union gunboats were still present the next morning, House would conclude that his ship had got away unobserved. House even had his own flag, white with a black disc in the center, which could be displayed by a runner carrying a cargo consigned to his warehouse.[85]

House's house flag got a lot of use. Like most private investors in blockade running, House imported as much as he could in the way of civilian consumer goods, knowing that these materials often brought a far higher profit than more basic necessities. In late February 1865, for example, the runner *Banshee (II)* made a daring daylight dash into Galveston through the middle of the Federal fleet (see Chapter 8). Soon after, a notice was published in the local papers "by order of T.W. House" announcing the auction of the ship's cargo. The March 21 sale was to include over 4,000 pairs of "linen trowsers," 4,800 pairs of women's stockings, lanterns, pots and pans, ten barrels of coffee and 150 boxes of whale oil candles. Two days after the sale, the *Houston Telegraph* reported that "as is generally the case in such heavy sales many goods brought all they were worth and others were sold at a heavy sacrifice." House also owned a stake in the screw steamer *Pelican*, which made one run into Galveston from Havana at the end of March 1865, and the side-wheel steamer *Jeanette*, which reportedly made two or three runs into Galveston from Havana.[86]

House also suffered some significant losses. His schooner *Mary Sorley*, captured by USS *Sciota* in April 1864 with 257 bales of cotton on board, brought gross proceeds of over $100,000 when she was auctioned at New Orleans that summer. House's losses were less with the schooner *Pet*, taken by boats' crews from *Bienville* and *Princess Royal* in February 1865 while anchored at San Luis Pass and auctioned for just under $20,000.[87]

Despite these losses, though, House's business instinct allowed him to shield himself from the financial calamity that devastated so many southerners at the end of the war. Like William Marsh Rice, House reportedly never trusted Confederate currency. Over the course of the war, he managed to stash away some $300,000 in gold with Baring's Brothers Bank in London, and still more had been deposited with his cotton agents in Liverpool.[88] This left House, in mid-1865, by far one of the wealthiest men in the region, "defeated but not dispossessed by the Civil War." After the war, House began buying up sugar plantations on the Texas coastal plain; by the time he died in 1880, House was said to have acquired 250,000 acres.[89]

At the beginning of the war, many in the South convinced themselves that by depriving European cotton markets of the white staple, they could draw France and (especially) Great Britain into the conflict on the side of the Confederacy, ensuring a quick and relatively clean break from the Union. So it was that through the early months of the war, when the Federal blockade of southern ports consisted of little more than a declaration on paper and maritime traffic could go in and out almost at will, the Confederacy adopted an unofficial policy of, in essence, blockading itself by withholding cotton shipments to foreign ports and waiting for the resulting clamor to bring the Europeans into the war. This approach, one that came to be known as "King Cotton" diplomacy, proved to be a disastrous miscalculation. Warehouses across the Atlantic were already jammed with southern cotton in 1861, and the British had begun expanding their own cotton-growing efforts around the Empire, notably in Egypt and India. King Cotton proved to be an imposing but ultimately impotent monarch, without the leverage to influence events much beyond the borders of his own realm.

Nevertheless, the new Confederate government in Richmond desperately needed money for its operations overseas for the purchase of munitions, uniforms and equipment and the construction of warships. By 1862, the Confederate government held large and increasing quantities of cotton but had no way to convert that into hard cash for use in Europe. In the winter of 1862–63, the Paris banking house of Emile Erlanger and Company began secret negotiations with the government in Richmond to issue bonds that would raise cash needed by Confederate agents working in Europe. The congress in Richmond passed a secret act authorizing Erlanger to issue £3,000,000 in bonds that would mature in twenty years. In the meantime, the bonds would generate an annual dividend of 7 percent, payable semiannually. Critically for the discussion of blockade running, the bonds were also redeemable for Confederate government cotton at six pence per pound "in the Confederacy itself."[90]

Erlanger published a prospectus for the bonds on March 19, 1863, offering them for sale through their agents in London, Liverpool, Amsterdam, Paris and Frankfurt. The bonds were sold at 90 percent of their face value, and initially there were far more subscribers than bonds available to supply them. The terms of sale were generous—5 percent down, another 10 percent when the bonds were issued and more installments after that. The open-market value of the Erlanger bonds rose briefly but then began a long, steady decline. The value dropped below the initial issue price of 90 percent by April 1, and the Erlanger Company began buying up its own bonds on the open market in an effort to sustain the price. This was a tactic that the company could not sustain, so Confederate agents in Europe signed a secret agreement with Erlanger to use the cash already generated by the sale of bonds to buy up more bonds, keeping the price high enough to encourage private investors to continue buying. To help keep the price up, Confederate agents like James Mason also encouraged rumors that the bonds would be honored no matter how the war ended. Thomas Dudley, the U.S. consul at Liverpool, was astonished. "As strange as it may seem," Dudley reported to Secretary of State Seward, "these people here who are aiding the Rebels and [have] taken or purchased these bonds think if worse comes and the Union is restored that the United States Government will assume the payment of their bonds." The Erlanger bond issue became a convoluted financial instrument with secret provisions that cut deeply into the amount of cash that was actually available for use in Europe by Confederate agents. One modern analysis of the program calculated that the entire effort netted £1,624,894 in cash—far below its nominal target of £3 million but nonetheless a very substantial amount of money for use by Confederate agents in Europe, who had few other options.[91]

The Erlanger effort also served as an important spur to blockade running in the Gulf of Mexico during the latter part of the war. Erlanger & Co. found itself, by mid-1863, holding a large number of its own bonds that it had quietly bought up on the open market in an effort to maintain the price. As bonds, they were of no tangible value to the company, but they also included a provision that allowed them to be exchanged for cotton within the Confederacy itself. Furthermore, the terms of the bond fixed the price at six pence (or about twelve U.S. cents) per pound of cotton, a fraction of what it commanded in the commodities markets of Paris, London and Liverpool. At the time the bonds were issued, a £1,000 Erlanger bond could be exchanged for cotton worth perhaps £4,000 on the British market, provided it could be gotten out of the Confederacy and to the United Kingdom. The opportunity for profit was even greater if the market price of cotton rose because the bonds-for-cotton exchange rate was fixed at six pence per pound.[92]

To exploit this opportunity, Erlanger partnered with its bond agent in the United Kingdom, banking house J.H. Schroeder & Co. of Manchester, and the H.O. Brewer Company of Mobile, Alabama, to form the European Trading Company, which would run cotton out of Mobile to Havana, Cuba.

Each entity brought with it a particular strength—Schroeder & Co. had the cash and connections in Britain, Brewer was a commission merchant of long standing in Mobile and Erlanger had a mountain of its own bonds that needed to be converted to cotton in the hold of a blockade runner bound for Cuba. To accomplish this, the European Trading Co. bought and operated four steamships: *Denbigh, Virgin, Vixen and Vulture*.[93]

The first and most successful of these—and the only one that ultimately would run into Texas—was the small, three-year-old, iron-hulled paddle steamer *Denbigh*, which had previously run between Liverpool and the nearby Welsh coastal town of Rhyl. *Denbigh* had been built at the Birkenhead shipyard of John Laird, Son & Co., across the River Mersey from Liverpool. At the time, Laird's yard was widely regarded as the most experienced in the United Kingdom, if not the world, in the construction of iron-hulled vessels. *Denbigh* shared several key features with newer, purpose-built runners launched on the Clyde, including a very long, narrow hull and shallow draft. *Denbigh* was known locally as a fast boat, having cut the usual passage time between Liverpool and Rhyl by about one-third, to one hour and forty minutes. Between May and September 1863, the ship went through a succession of owners, finally ending up in the hands of one Clotworthy Boyd of London for £6,500, substantially less than her cost to build just a few years before. While Boyd remained the owner of record for the rest of *Denbigh*'s career, he was almost certainly a "godfather," as William Watson would have called him, whose role was to disguise the true ownership of the vessel and the nature of her new business.[94]

To command the new runner, the European Trading Company selected Francis McNevin, a thirty-four-year-old Jerseyman. McNevin was a veteran mariner, having obtained his Extra Master Certificate of Competency, the highest grade of licensure issued by the British Board of Trade, in 1854, while he was still in his mid-twenties. His voyages in the decade since had carried him from the East Indies and the Mediterranean to the west coast of Africa and ports on the U.S. Atlantic and Gulf seaboards. As his first mate, McNevin selected Edward Scandrett, a forty-year-old Welshman who had served on some of the same ships as McNevin, though apparently at different times. McNevin also took care to bring with him aboard *Denbigh* a cook and steward from his previous ship. In all, twenty-two men formed the crew of *Denbigh* on October 19, 1863, when she set out across the Atlantic for Bermuda and, beyond that, Havana and Mobile.[95]

Their departure did not go unnoticed. Thomas Dudley, the U.S. consul at Liverpool, maintained a network of informants who kept him apprised

Digital reconstruction of the blockade runner *Denbigh. Author's illustration.*

of activities in that port. Dudley forwarded detailed reports on suspected blockade runners through State Department channels to be passed along to the navy. Dudley's report for October 1863 included a detailed description of the *Denbigh*'s physical appearance. Dudley also noted that a man named Abner M. Godfrey, "late coal agent for the Confederates at Cardiff," and his wife were aboard the ship and that Godfrey "is said to be the owner of the *Denbigh*."[96] In fact, Godfrey was undoubtedly traveling as *supercargo*, the onboard representative of the ship's actual owners, the European Trading Co. Although Godfrey was not a blue-water mariner of great experience, he was a "bayman" who had spent many years before the war in Mobile and was well qualified to serve as both the ship's business manager and pilot at that port. Consul Dudley was right to be concerned about *Denbigh*; under Captain McNevin and, later, Godfrey himself, she would go on to make a name as one of the most successful runners of the war, the bane of the Union's West Gulf Blockading Squadron.

Chapter 7
PRIZE MONEY

*Visions of enormous amounts of prize-money now began to dance through the
brains of the excited officers and crew as they gathered at the rail of the ship,
watching the movements and waiting for the return of the boarding officer and the
report of his investigation.*
—*Israel Everett Vail,* Three Years on the Blockade

One important inducement for Union sailors was prize money. When
a ship or other suspected enemy property was captured, the officers
and enlisted crew members of the seizing vessel were entitled to a share
of the cash value of the enemy ship, or "prize." The awarding of prize
money was part of a long tradition in Europe and, later, in the U.S. Navy.
When a suspect vessel was taken, its captors would put a skeleton crew on
board to sail it to the nearest U.S. admiralty court for adjudication. For ships
seized off the Texas coast, that was usually at New Orleans or Key West.
There, the navy would present a "libel" against the prize, evidence that the
vessel had, in fact, been caught running in or out of a blockaded southern
port. The ship's papers would be entered into the record, along with cargo
manifests, logbooks and other records. Often one or more of the captured
ship's officers or crew would be brought in to give testimony as well.

The seized ship's owners, or their representatives, were also permitted to
present evidence of their own to show that the seizure had been unwarranted.
Sometimes these challenges were successful on first hearing or, like any other
legal case, were drawn out interminably by appeals that might go as high

U.S. Navy boat's ensign used during the Civil War. *U.S. Naval History and Heritage Command.*

as the U.S. Supreme Court. It was not unusual for prize cases during the Civil War to drag on for many months or even years. Even when a case was quickly adjudicated and prize money assigned for allotment, it could be a very long time before the men entitled actually received their share. Francis Davenport, a former officer on USS *Portsmouth*, writing long after the war about the first prize his ship had captured, noted laconically, "I think I got some $43 prize money about twelve years afterward…"[97]

In most cases the seizure was upheld by the court and the vessel and all its contents were inventoried, appraised and put up for auction. After deductions for court costs and inventorying, appraising and auctioning the prize, half the proceeds was retained by the government and placed in a fund for disabled seamen, while the other half was divvied up between the officers and crew of the squadron that made the capture. The admiral commanding the regional squadron (e.g., the West Gulf Blockading Squadron) collected 5 percent of the total proceeds, the local commodore received 1 percent and the remaining 44 percent was split among the officers and men of the naval vessel(s) that had actually made the capture. In keeping with a U.S. law dating to 1800, the captain and officers aboard the capturing vessels claimed the lion's share of the prize money, while the far more numerous enlisted sailors and Marines were left to divide a small part of the proceeds among themselves.[98]

Estimates of the total value of prizes captured during the war range as high as $31 million. Though an individual seaman's share might be small, prize money remained an important inducement to service and helped make some officers wealthy. By collecting 5 percent of the value of each prize taken by their regional squadrons, some senior admirals were believed to have pocketed small fortunes during their appointments. Samuel Phillips Lee, who commanded the North Atlantic Blockading Squadron off Wilmington, North Carolina, reportedly referred to his post as the "prize money command." Lee was so protective of his perquisite that he hired his own attorney, acting on commission, to represent him in prize cases. The lawyer did his job well, helping Lee to collect $109,689.99 in prize money during his two years' tenure in command, the highest of any Union officer.[99] Perhaps the most avaricious of Union naval commanders—at least by reputation—was David Dixon Porter, commander of the navy's Mississippi River Squadron. Though his river gunboats were operating hundreds of miles from the sea, in 1863 Porter issued an order to his squadron extending the conventional navy prize rules to the seizure of any property belonging to the enemy. Landing parties from the Mississippi Squadron's gunboats scoured plantations, groves and barns miles from the river, rounding up cotton to be shipped north and adjudicated at Cairo, Illinois. Porter's actions interfered with the work of the Treasury Department and civilian merchants licensed by the Lincoln administration to trade in cotton, so the Navy Department eventually put an end to Porter's shady game—but not before the admiral's 5 percent share had netted him thousands of dollars and his officers and enlisted men many tens of thousands more.[100]

There were not a great many lucrative prizes to be found off the Texas coast, but over the course of the war, the Union navy snatched up prizes on a regular basis. Most of these were small sailing vessels carrying a few tons of assorted cargo inbound or fifty to seventy-five bales of cotton outbound. Typical of these was the British schooner *Fanny*, captured off the mouth of the Brazos River by USS *Owasco* in April 1864. *Fanny* was sent with a prize crew to New Orleans, where the schooner and her cargo of assorted goods were condemned by the court and auctioned for a total of $10,317.61. After deductions for court expenses, payment of half the remaining proceeds to the disabled seamen's fund and the senior officers' cut, some $4,044.46 remained to be divided among *Owasco*'s officers and crew. Under the prize regulations, the blockader's commanding officer, Lieutenant Commander E.W. Henry, would have collected a share of just over $600, while the ordinary seamen and Marines aboard *Owasco* would have eventually pocketed about $10 each.[101]

The prize game was nothing if not fickle, though. Just three weeks later, on the very same stretch of water, *Owasco*'s sister ship *Chocura* made a

A U.S. Navy gunboat typical of the small blockading vessels used in the Gulf of Mexico. *Illustration by Captain Byng, from Watson's* The Adventures of a Blockade Runner, *1892.*

double capture that proved to be one of the most lucrative involving sailing runners on the Texas coast. Late on the evening of May 2, 1864, *Chocura* was anchored off the mouth of the Brazos, watching for runners trying to move in or out of the river. Around 11:40 p.m., the lookouts reported a strange sail standing out to sea, and *Chocura's* captain, Bancroft Gherardi, ordered his crew to slip the anchor cable and give chase. He caught up with the schooner in about thirty-five minutes; a boarding party discovered the vessel to be the British schooner *Agnes*, loaded with cotton. No sooner had Gherardi begun transferring a prize crew to the schooner than his lookout reported seeing a light farther to the south. *Chocura* quickly cast off from the first prize and began churning southward into the darkness in pursuit of the second vessel. Gherardi caught up with her about twenty-five miles offshore. She proved to be the Prussian schooner *Frederic the Second*, loaded with 114 bales of cotton, which had run out of the Brazos along with *Agnes*. Gherardi put a second prize crew aboard *Frederic the Second* and sent both schooners off to New Orleans for adjudication.[102]

Gherardi and his crew were lucky in capturing two cotton-laden schooners within the space of a few hours, but they were luckier still in the timing of their prize case. When the prize court ruled in favor of *Chocura's* seizure and ordered *Agnes*, *Frederic the Second* and their cargoes to be auctioned in the fall of 1864, speculation and other factors had driven the price of cotton at New Orleans to a record high of $1.00 or more per pound. The two schooners and their contents together fetched a remarkable $131,295.28. After deductions for court costs and the usual division of funds, Bancroft Gherardi would have collected just over $8,000.00, while the lowliest ship's boy probably received around $225.00, nearly a year's pay for an ordinary seaman.[103]

Sometimes an even bigger prize slipped through the captors' fingers. On May 28, 1864, lookouts aboard USS *Admiral* spotted a steamship trying to run into Galveston. *Admiral* was not much of a warship, having been bought into the navy for use as a supply vessel. Nevertheless, *Admiral*'s commanding officer, William Eaton, immediately set out in chase of the strange vessel whose master, Eaton later reported, "handled her with great skill and desperate courage." After a six-hour chase, *Admiral* managed to get close enough to fire two broadsides into the mysterious steamer. Still the ship carried on, until small-arms fire from the Marines aboard *Admiral* forced the steamship's crew to abandon the ship's wheel and take cover below deck. One of the runner's officers, a man named John Davis, was severely injured in the gunfire to the extent that he later had his left arm and three fingers of his right hand amputated by *Admiral*'s surgeon.[104]

Once aboard the captured steamer, the blockaders discovered why her master, a man named Blake, had put up such a desperate chase; her holds were crammed with military supplies, including gunpowder, small arms, boxes of percussion caps and medicines. The ship's capture was satisfying as well because she turned out to be the steamer *Isabel*, "an old offender" that had earned "much notoriety" running between Havana, Mobile and Galveston.[105] Just weeks before, *Isabel* had been one of the two steamers that escaped with *Lavinia* (ex-*Harriet Lane*) from Galveston right under the noses of the blockading fleet that was specifically on the lookout for them (see Chapter 4). That episode had been an abject embarrassment for the Federals, so the capture of one of those vessels with a cargo of munitions must have been seen as a sort of delayed retribution.

Not surprisingly, given both the size and symbolism of *Isabel*'s capture, two other Union warships, *Kanawha* and *Kineo*, also claimed a share. (*Kineo* had been present when *Isabel* and the others escaped from Galveston on April 30.) Lieutenant Commander B.B. Taylor of *Kanawha* outlined his ship's claim to a share of the prize, reporting that he had witnessed the entire action, "seeing distinctly the flash of the guns and the bursting of the shells…and at the time the last gun was fired and the vessel surrendered the *Kanawha* was less than 5 miles distant from the *Admiral* and her prize and within easy signal distance." The commander of *Kineo*, John Watters, made a similar claim to having witnessed the fight and exchanged signals with both *Admiral* and *Kanawha*, justifying his ship's share in the prize. Each captain's claim to being within signal distance of *Admiral* was critical because prize regulations laid out that all ships within signaling range should share equally in the prize, whether they actively participated in the action or not. But it was not to be. Unbeknownst to Eaton and the others, during the fight that led to her capture, *Isabel* had been holed by "three or four shots [that] had hit her between wind and water," and she was leaking badly by the time she reached the Mississippi River with her prize crew. She sank in the Mississippi on the night of June 2–3. Two ship's boats and some of her cargo (including a crate of absinthe) were salvaged and ultimately auctioned off for about $20,000, but the rest was a total loss. Eaton tried to put the best face on it in his report to the Navy Department, admitting that while he was disappointed at the loss of the prize money, he was also "gratified and consoled in the fact of having discharged my duty by destroying a vessel celebrated in the Gulf above all others of her class."[106]

The commanding officer of the West Gulf Blockading Squadron during this period, David Farragut, would have appreciated Lieutenant Eaton's commitment to the destruction of runners even when it meant the loss of prize money. As a regional squadron commander, Farragut himself stood to gain substantially from the 5 percent share on all prizes taken by the squadron, but he repeatedly expressed his displeasure with what he saw as a tendency for some captains under his command to abandon a chase to stop and pick up what he termed "waif cotton"—bales that had been thrown overside from runners trying to lighten their ships. Union ships picking up this cotton often claimed it under the rules of civilian salvage, as if it had randomly appeared in their path, with an unknown origin—hence the term "waif." This legal fiction would entitle them to all of the proceeds rather than having to share them with the government and their senior officers. In May 1864, Farragut issued a general order to all ships in his command, reminding them that "all cotton or other merchandise picked up at sea or on shore must be taken into port and delivered up to the United States courts for adjudication, as though it had been captured, in order that the judicial authorities may distribute it as prize or award salvage to the captors."[107]

The admiral might have had in mind an egregious case that occurred in the squadron the previous summer, when the U.S. bark *William G. Anderson* captured the schooner *America* north of the Rio Grande. The prize capsized and sank while under tow, and *Anderson*'s commander, Lieutenant Frederic S.

Hill, reported recovering thirteen bags of cotton. That was not true; Hill's crew had recovered forty additional bales, amounting to something like *ten tons* of dry cotton, which they quietly sent to New York for sale through civilian channels. Lieutenant Hill was court-martialed and convicted of "scandalous conduct tending to the destruction of good morals," but his sentence amounted to a reprimand and a relatively small fine.[108] That lenient punishment suggests that the court did not find his transgression to be too serious and that actions like Hill's may have been more commonplace than was generally acknowledged.

Chapter 8
NARROW ESCAPES AND SHOAL WATERS

We nearly had the Denbigh...*He is a bold rascal, and well he may be, for if I get him he will see the rest of his days of the war in the Tortugas.*
— *Union rear admiral David Glasgow Farragut, 1864*

The citizens of Mobile, Alabama, awoke on the gray, overcast morning of Friday, August 5, 1864, to the low rumble of distant gunfire away to the south. First, there were a few isolated shots, then an almost continuous roar that could be felt as much as heard. No one needed to ask his neighbor the cause, as everyone must surely have guessed it: the U.S. Navy had begun its long-awaited entrance to Mobile Bay, engaging with the heavy guns of Forts Morgan and Gaines, thirty miles to the south.

The ships of Admiral Farragut's West Gulf Blockading Squadron steamed steadily up into the entrance of the bay in pairs, the larger wooden warships lashed together with the smaller, which were positioned on the port side and somewhat protected from the big guns of Fort Morgan. The main column was led by USS *Brooklyn*, now commanded by James Alden, the same officer who had instituted the blockade at Galveston three years before. To the starboard of this column, closest to both Fort Morgan and a field of underwater obstructions and mines, steamed four monitors of the U.S. Navy's newest class of armored warships.

The leading monitor, USS *Tecumseh*, struck a mine near the fort and, having little reserve buoyancy, rolled over and sank in less than two minutes, taking most of her crew with her. The other Union ships pressed on, past the entrance channel and into the lower reaches of Mobile Bay, where they engaged the Confederate ironclad *Tennessee*. By 10:00 a.m., the fight was over—*Tennessee* had struck her colors, and Farragut had secured the entrance to Mobile Bay. Forts Gaines and Morgan, guarding the western and eastern approaches to the bay, respectively, would surrender within days. While Mobile itself would not surrender until April 1865, the city's days as a blockade-running port ended with the last echoes of gunfire from the Battle of Mobile Bay.

The closure of Mobile to blockade runners beginning in August 1864 was a significant development in several respects. Strategically, it shut down the last significant Confederate port in the Gulf of Mexico east of the Mississippi River. While Mobile was a long distance from the battlefields of the eastern theater of the war, it remained connected by rail, and at least some of the Confederate government consignments brought into that port were being quickly directed to other parts of the Confederacy by the chief military quartermaster in Richmond.[109] Farragut's victory at Mobile Bay closed that important point of resupply permanently.

The loss of Mobile also gave Texas, and Galveston in particular, new importance as a blockade-running destination. Relatively few steam blockade runners attempted Texas harbors during the first three years of the war, but after August 1864, Galveston remained the only significant port on the Gulf of Mexico in Confederate hands. Although Texas was largely isolated from the rest of the Confederacy, after Mobile Bay, Galveston stood with only Wilmington, North Carolina, and Charleston, South Carolina, as a port with active blockade-running operations. After February 1865, Galveston would stand alone.

Among the first runners to arrive at Galveston after the fall of Mobile Bay were *Susanna*, around August 24, 1864, and the European Trading Co.'s steamship *Denbigh*, on August 25. *Denbigh* had been the last steamship to slip out of Mobile before Farragut's attack, and her arrivals and departures there— seven round voyages between Havana and Mobile in all—had seemed so regular and reliable that people began calling her "the packet." U.S. Secretary of the Navy Gideon Welles dryly noted this, writing to Farragut that "for some time past her arrival [at Mobile], when due, has been looked for with the same degree of certainty of any steamer regularly running to this port, and so far she has not disappointed expectations." Under Captain Francis McNevin, and subsequently under Abner Godfrey, *Denbigh* developed a reputation for cheeky insolence that irritated the Union naval officers tasked with her capture. It didn't help their mood that *Denbigh* was by then understood to be a relatively

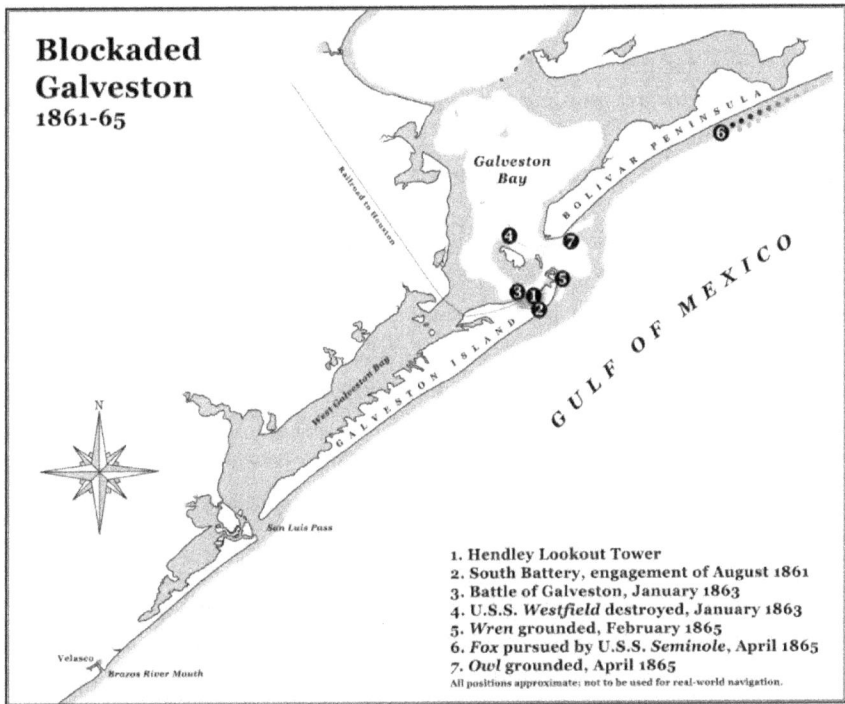

Blockaded Galveston 1861-65

Galveston Bay

GULF OF MEXICO

N

San Luis Pass

Velasco

Brazos River Mouth

1. Hendley Lookout Tower
2. South Battery, engagement of August 1861
3. Battle of Galveston, January 1863
4. U.S.S. *Westfield* destroyed, January 1863
5. *Wren* grounded, February 1865
6. *Fox* pursued by U.S.S. *Seminole*, April 1865
7. *Owl* grounded, April 1865
All positions approximate; not to be used for real-world navigation.

Galveston, Texas, and vicinity. *Original map by the author.*

slow ship and got in and out of Mobile more by stealth than speed. Farragut blustered that he would send *Denbigh*'s master to rot in the U.S. military prison at Fort Jefferson, in the Dry Tortugas, if he caught him. On one occasion, when the blockaders believed that they'd forced *Denbigh* aground near the entrance to Mobile Bay, Farragut's flag captain, Percival Drayton, wrote to a colleague that "if the *Denbigh* is not destroyed to-night I trust that we will keep the Fourth [of July] by going in and doing it with our broadside. This long howl business is mere vanity and waste of shot."[110]

In the fall of 1864, with the Confederacy clearly tottering and the time to make a fortune running short, some men entered the blockade-running game who had no business being at sea, let alone trying to sneak past vigilant Yankee gunboats. William Watson, the Scotsman who had begun the war as a Confederate soldier and later ran the blockade into Texas in his schooner *Rob Roy*, observed that by early 1865, "the general scramble [at Galveston] seemed to have become more desperate, and blockade running was now carried on to a reckless degree."[111]

In the winter of 1864–65, a number of runners that had previously gone into Confederate ports on the Atlantic seaboard shifted their operations to running between Havana and Galveston. One of these was *Will o' the Wisp*, the Clyde-built side-wheel steamer that Tom Taylor had been running into Wilmington, North Carolina. Although *Wisp* had made considerable profits for Taylor's employer, the Anglo-Confederate Trading Company, the ship had also proved to be mechanically unreliable and structurally unsound. In October 1864, Taylor succeeded in passing her off to new owners, who brought her into the Gulf of Mexico.[112]

Sometime in December 1864 *Will o' the Wisp* successfully ran into Galveston, where she took on a load of cotton and several women and children intending to travel to Havana. Under the command of Abner M. Godfrey, who had come out to Havana on *Denbigh*, she slipped out of Galveston again around January 10, 1865, but was soon overtaken by a ferocious gale that lasted four days. It was a hard journey for Godfrey's passengers:

> *For some days and nights they all were much frightened, the gale blowing very heavy. I tried to cheer and console them all I could, but it was a hard matter to make them confident…Say to Mr. Gregory that his little daughter is a perfect heroine. Finally all the ladies were of very good courage considering the trials they were called upon to undergo. I hope they may never again be obliged to encounter such scrapes as those upon our late unfortunate passage.*[113]

By the time the storm ended, the steamer was very short of coal, and Godfrey made for the nearest port available—Sisal on the Yucatán coast. *Wisp* limped into Sisal on January 16, almost out of coal. Godfrey landed his passengers at Sisal and "left them in comfortable apartments" there, pending his planned return later in the month. After purchasing twenty-two tons of coal from the steamship *Tabasco*, Godfrey set out for Vera Cruz, 350 nautical miles to the west, where he could refit the side-wheeler. To save coal, he ran the ship on only one of her four boilers, at the most economical speed possible. Nevertheless, Godfrey almost didn't make it:

> [I] *just reached* [Vera Cruz] *by burning up my hawsers, fenders and everything that could be raised about the decks, even to coal bags; and to succeed in getting over the bar, burnt up all the pork and bacon on board ship. Had we been out one hour longer,* [we] *must have lost the steamer, as she must have went ashore on the reefs.*[114]

Destruction of *Will o' the Wisp. Author's illustration.*

At Vera Cruz, Godfrey turned over command of *Wisp* to one of his officers, a man named Stockton, who sailed again on January 30 for Galveston. On Friday evening, February 3, while running northeastward in a fog along the Galveston Island shore toward the Southwest Channel, *Will o' the Wisp* was spotted by one of the blockaders, which opened fire on the side-wheeler. That shot missed, and *Wisp* disappeared into the fog once again. But in evading the blockader, *Wisp* ran aground several miles south of the city. The ship stuck fast, and the crew clambered down into the surf. They were met on the beach by Confederate sentries, who initially suspected them of being a Federal landing party. The crew eventually made it to the home of a man named Middlegger, who gave them something to eat and let them bed down for the night.[115]

Over the next several days, the stranded ship was swarmed by Confederate soldiers and civilians, as well as the party formally assigned to salvage the cargo. The ship, according to a Union officer who later went on board, was "so near the beach as to require but a plank, which was there, for the rebels to board her."[116] Most of the cargo was stolen by soldiers or civilians, either for their own use or in hopes of being able to sell to others. After the fog

Salvage of the blockade runner *Ruby* near Charleston, South Carolina, in 1863. The salvage work done on *Acadia* and *Will o' the Wisp* would have looked much like this, with machinery components carefully disassembled, sorted and stacked on the beach for removal. *Library of Congress.*

lifted on February 6, two Union warships discovered the stranded steamer and shelled her for about two hours, but by then the vessel had been picked clean. In the predawn darkness of February 10, a week after *Wisp* went aground, boarding parties from USS *Princess Royal* and USS *Antona* went aboard to destroy what was left, but they needn't have bothered. "The vessel was completely riddled in her hull from our fire on a previous occasion," the commander of *Princess Royal* wrote in his report. "Her hold was full of sand and water; her after section awash, and the deck scuttled fore and aft, for the purpose, apparently, of getting out her cargo. The engine had been taken to pieces, and the vessel was a complete wreck. The wheelhouses were the only part which could be burned...Everything [else] was destroyed excepting what was under water and beyond reach."[117] The small part of the cargo that was successfully salvaged—estimated later to be about one-tenth of the total—was consigned to Thomas W. House, who included it ("slightly damaged") in a big auction of "blockade importations" on February 28 in Houston. Lots recovered from *Wisp* included plate tin, Brazilian coffee, "gents' half hose" and sixty reams of paper.[118]

At the same time soldiers and civilians were picking over the wreck of *Will o' the Wisp*, the runner *Acadia* ended her brief life on the Gulf beach about forty miles south of Galveston. *Acadia* had been launched at Sorel (now Sorel-Tracy), Quebec, on the St. Lawrence River in May 1864. She was a large side-wheel steamer, 211 feet long and registered at 738 tons. There was little infrastructure for the construction of iron-hulled vessels in Canada at the time, so *Acadia* was built of timber. *Acadia* was registered at Montreal on the last day of October 1864 by Jacques Felix Lincennes of Sorel and William McNaughton of Montreal, but her true ownership remains unclear. *Acadia*'s owners evidently intended to run her through the blockade or otherwise dispose of the ship to make a quick profit because they took the step of noting on her registry papers that her master, Thomas Leach, was empowered to sell the ship with "no minimum price named, at any place out of the province of Canada."[119]

Acadia sailed from Halifax for Nassau on December 6, 1864. Among her passengers was a group of men who the local U.S. consul reported were part of a "piratical gang" of Confederates traveling to Vera Cruz, Mexico, from there to go overland to California with the intent of seizing a U.S. Mail steamer on the Pacific coast. *Acadia* made a brief stop at Nassau, where she took on cargo for Texas, and then another at Havana, loading more inbound cargo. After a stop at Vera Cruz to land the Confederates bound for California, *Acadia* sailed again, this time setting a northerly course for the Texas coast.[120]

Acadia ran hard aground in the surf between San Luis Pass and the mouth of the Brazos River around dusk on February 5, 1865, in the same heavy fog conditions that led to the loss of *Wisp*. Captain Leach—who by some accounts was trying to enter the mouth of the Brazos River at Velasco (an ill-conceived plan if true, given the large size of the steamer)—later claimed that he had intended to reach the coast much farther north, about fifteen miles south of Galveston, but had been pushed off course by a strong current. In fact, *Acadia*'s failed attempt to run the blockade seems in retrospect to have been almost doomed by incompetence. The ship's sailing master, frustrated at his inability to get his bearings in the fog, had reportedly given up charge of piloting the vessel before the ship struck bottom, and the steamer's magnetic compass had allegedly never been properly secured or adjusted, "no regard being had for quantity of iron and iron nails closely connected with the needle, in fact, not a binnacle in the ship, the compasses not even fixed on deck when leaving Havana." The destruction of the ship was made complete the following morning, when she was discovered and shelled by the blockader USS *Virginia*.[121]

Much of *Acadia*'s cargo was salvaged by the Confederates and sold at auction in Houston later in February, bringing in over $28,000. The lots, as reported by the *Galveston Weekly News*, included flannel cloth, Nova Scotia wool, linen and silk handkerchiefs, lead pencils, letter paper and envelopes, percussion caps, hand tools, preserved fruit, black tea, claret, playing cards, gold lace, French quinine and calomel. Also included was a quantity of "blue mass," a mercury-based medicinal used to treat everything from constipation and syphilis to tuberculosis and birthing pain. The editor of the *Weekly News* was fairly disgusted at the premium paid for luxury items, even as the Confederacy was entering its death throes: "The few dozen preserved fruits…brought from four to five hundred per cent on first cost, while the necessary articles of iron brought but 10¢, but a trifle over actual cost, showing a proneness to indulge our appetites in preference to supplying the actual wants of the country."[122]

Two large blockade runners being wrecked and destroyed within forty-eight hours of each other was suspicious; then it was learned that the runner *Wren* had briefly run aground off the entrance to Galveston harbor. *Wren* escaped, but rumors about saboteurs were in the air:

> *There is hardly any room to doubt that the three* [sic] *steamers were wrecked on our coast by Yankees in disguise…We should never forget that treachery, falsehood and deception are the peculiar characteristics of Yankees, and we*

believe we have more to fear from these traits than from all their power in open and honorable war...The coast of Texas is the safest of any on the whole seaboard of this continent. The water shoals so gradually and so uniformly that, with the lead line in the hands of any but a Yankee, no blockade runner could be beached in the thickest fog, unless intentionally. We have no doubt that the loss of the Wisp, *the* Wren *and the* Arcadia [sic] *is due to Yankee treachery.*[123]

The newspaper editor's fear of "Yankee treachery" notwithstanding, there is no evidence that these incidents were caused by anything other than navigation errors in terrible weather conditions; similar groundings had happened before, and more would happen later.

In fact, it was during these final months of the conflict that blockade running at Galveston by steamships peaked. The capture of Fort Fisher, North Carolina, in January 1865 and the surrender of Charleston in February effectively closed the last significant Confederate ports on the Atlantic seaboard, leaving Galveston alone as a destination for the big steam runners. Although Texas was too far removed from the center of the war for arms and munitions brought into Texas to make a difference in the outcome of the conflict, there was still money to be made.

Three weeks after *Will o' the Wisp* went aground, her former agent, Tom Taylor, ran the blockade into Galveston aboard one of the Anglo-Confederate Trading Company's other ships, *Banshee (II)*. This big steamer made a total of four round voyages into Confederate ports—three into Wilmington and one into Galveston.[124]

This last Galveston trip was harrowing for both Taylor and the ship's crew. They arrived off the entrance to Galveston on a relatively calm, dark night and began creeping their way through the blockaders. The weather quickly changed to "a regular 'Norther,'" with torrents of rain followed by heavy gusts of cold wind from the north and northwest. The wind blew so hard that *Banshee (II)* could not make any headway against it, and Captain Jonathan W. Steele allowed the ship to drift to leeward toward the open sea. After drifting clear of the Union fleet, *Banshee (II)* set a course to the westward, making landfall again about thirty miles southwest of Galveston. The winds subsided, and the big steamer remained anchored in shallow water through the following day, keeping a close watch out for patrolling Federal gunboats. *Banshee (II)* got under way again around dusk, slowly steaming up the coast to make another attempt at the entrance. Along the way, they passed the wreck of *Wisp*, which Taylor recognized "as our old friend...which had been driven ashore and lost on the very first trip [*sic*] she made after I had sold her."[125]

Banshee (II) anchored several miles from the entrance to the harbor. Captain Steele raised anchor and began moving again about two hours before daylight on February 24. The plan was to be well inside the cordon of Union gunboats before first light and make a quick dash through the Southwest Channel. Unfortunately, they came very close to running down a launch filled with Yankee sailors, one of those sent out every night to fill gaps in the Federals' line of blockade ships (see Chapter 5). *Banshee (II)* continued on, cranking up to full speed as the stunned Yankee sailors began shooting off "rocket after rocket in our wake as a warning to the blockading fleet to be on the alert."[126]

With any chance of stealth now gone, Captain Steele charged headlong for the entrance to the bay. They had badly misjudged their earlier position, though, and instead of finding themselves inside the Union fleet as the sun crept over the horizon, they discovered they were still three or four miles from town. The entire Federal squadron lay ahead. Taylor and Steele decided to press on. Now it was light enough that the blockaders, previously alerted to the runner's presence, could train their guns on the big side-wheeler. But Taylor and Steele had two factors in their favor. Being in the Southwest Channel, the shallows to seaward of them prevented the Union gunboats from getting any closer than a half mile. The shoal between the contestants also kept the water relatively calm inside the channel, while the rougher water outside made it difficult for the gunboats to lay their fire accurately. On *Banshee (II)* ran, with Federal shells whistling overhead and splashing into the water around them as leadsmen on either side continually tested the depth of the water:

> It was not a question of the fathoms, but of the feet; we were drawing twelve feet, ten, nine, and when we put her at it as you do a horse at a jump, and as her nose was entering the white water, "eight feet" was sung out. A moment afterwards we touched and hung, and I thought all was over when a big wave came rolling along and lifted our stern and the ship bodily with a crack which could be heard a quarter of a mile off, and which we thought meant that her back was broken.[127]

The steel-hulled runner was not fatally damaged, though, and after two or three more hard thumps on the sand, she passed into the deeper water of the harbor entrance beyond. Taylor recalled that after being cleared by the port's health officer, *Banshee (II)* "steamed gaily up to the town, the wharves of which were crowded by people who, gazing to seaward, had watched our exploit with much interest, and who cheered us heartily upon its success." The steamer sailed again later in March, eventually reaching Nassau on March 30 with one thousand bales of cotton.[128]

Through the first four months of 1865, steam blockade runners continued to arrive at Galveston at the rate of about one a week—at least twenty arrivals in all.[129] A few ships, like *Denbigh* and *Lark*, made multiple round voyages between Havana and Galveston during that period. Mostly these ships ran in and out again without being spotted, but it was becoming a much more hazardous game than it had been before. In addition to the ordinary perils of navigation, as exemplified by the loss of *Will o' the Wisp* and *Acadia*, the number of Federal warships assigned to the blockade grew steadily as other Confederate ports fell, freeing up gunboats assigned there to be moved to the West Gulf Blockading Squadron.

William Watson made one final trip into Galveston in the closing days of the war. In March 1865 he was in Havana, having recently sold his schooner *Rob Roy*, when he was recruited to sail aboard the new runner *Pelican*, under contract to Houston merchant Thomas W. House. The master who had brought *Pelican* across the Atlantic had stepped down, not wanting to run the blockade, and the new captain "had not much experience at sea, and knew nothing of navigation." Watson agreed to go along and serve as navigator and pilot for getting in and out of Galveston.[130]

Watson looked over the ship, a twin-screw steamer, and assessed *Pelican* to be "tolerably well found" to the task. Her master's charts were badly out of date, though, so Watson brought his own, which he had extensively annotated during his own voyages.[131]

While the twenty officers and crew seemed capable enough, only two men besides Watson had ever run the blockade before. Their inexperience revealed itself almost immediately after leaving Havana, when the master sent a ship's boy around to light the ship's running lights for the night. The master seemed genuinely dumbfounded at Watson's insistence that this was a case where the regulations had to be ignored, but he complied and had the lights extinguished.[132]

On the third evening out, when approaching the Texas coast, *Pelican* was sighted and chased briefly by a Union gunboat, but Watson employed a standard runner's trick, opening the furnace dampers to produce a huge volume of black, greasy smoke in the ship's wake. Then, cutting off the smoke suddenly, Watson made a sharp change in *Pelican*'s course, leaving the

Union ship to continue steering for the dark smudge on the horizon. *Pelican* later resumed her original course, making landfall several miles southwest of Galveston, and began creeping slowly along the shore, headed for the Southwest Channel that ran along the Galveston beach. Eventually Watson spotted the signal light atop Hendley's Row, "not far off, but dim, probably from the scarcity of oil."[133]

Watson was worried that *Pelican*, light-draft as she was, would still find herself aground in the shallowest part of the channel, as the water was now at ebb tide. His concern proved to be correct, and *Pelican* grounded not far from the battery at Fort Point. At this point, they were well inshore of the blockaders, and with the tide rising, the ship floated free again in about an hour. *Pelican* continued slowly on her way up the channel and by 2:00 a.m. was anchored near the Confederate guard boat, waiting for the boarding officer to inspect the ship's papers.[134]

Just after William Watson's arrival in *Pelican* occurred one of the more remarkable incidents of the blockade on the Texas coast. The British paddle steamer *Fox* was one of several purpose-built blockade runners that appeared in the Gulf during the last months of the war. Built of steel, she was long and lean, measuring 219 feet between perpendiculars (about 230 feet overall), with a beam of just 22 feet. *Fox* was a very successful blockade runner, having made eight round voyages between Nassau and Charleston before entering the Gulf of Mexico and running into Galveston. *Fox*'s master was Simpson Adkins, an experienced pilot on the Carolina coast. Adkins was an old hand at running the blockade and well known to the Federal navy. He was captured at least twice and both times returned to his old calling upon release. After his second capture, a Federal officer described Adkins as an "old offender" and "one of the most expert pilots on the Southern coast."[135] The officer warned his colleagues to watch Adkins carefully, but it did no good—by 1865, he was back running the blockade again, this time to Galveston.

Before dawn on April 1, *Fox* was moving along under easy steam, some eighty miles offshore, probably looking to make landfall north of Galveston and wait until nightfall to run past the Union fleet. The growing light in the east, though, revealed the silhouette of a Federal gunboat patrolling the distant approaches to the coast. A column of black smoke soon appeared over the gunboat, USS *Preston*, at that point lying about eight miles astern of *Fox*, as the Yankees poured on coal to give chase. Adkins and his pilot, a "quiet, self-possessed and fearless" Galveston man named Harry Wachsen, recognized they had little chance getting to seaward without being cut off

A sketch of the runner *Fox*, made at Bermuda. *St. Georges Museum, Bermuda, via U.S. Navy.*

Contemporary sketch of USS *Seminole*. *Library of Congress.*

by their pursuer, so they set their course west toward a point on the Bolivar Peninsula some miles north of Galveston, where they hoped they could stay out of sight of the main Union fleet.[136]

Both ships were now pounding toward shore as fast as they could, across a wide expanse of Gulf, still well beyond sight of land. *Fox* was carrying in her holds lead, iron implements, barrels of beef and other very heavy articles; Adkins had the hatches opened and these things dropped overboard to lighten the ship.

On and on the ships raced until the shore was in plain sight ahead of *Fox*. Aboard the blockaders anchored off Galveston, it was yet a routine Saturday morning, with crews at work scrubbing the decks, touching up paintwork and polishing brass. At about 10:00 a.m., on USS *Seminole*, Marine sergeant John Freeman Mackie heard a lookout at the masthead cry, "Sail ho!" Signals were passed to the squadron flagship, *Ossipee*, and soon a second vessel was spotted, this one "a long low steamer about eight miles to the eastward, burning black smoke, steaming rapidly to the northward and westward." The squadron commander, Captain John Guest, ordered *Seminole* to intercept this second ship, which later proved to be Adkins's *Fox*.[137]

Aboard the runner, Adkins and Wachsen spotted the Union ships at about the same time and altered course to starboard. They were now headed full-speed at a right angle toward the beach. *Seminole* was closing, though, so Adkins altered his course again, to almost due north, and set out a pair of small sails to add a little extra speed. Captain Albert G. Clary of *Seminole* was ready for this maneuver and shouted orders to set the ship's fore and main topsails, along with jibs and staysails. "In a minute," Mackie later recalled, "the *Seminole* was staggering under a cloud of canvas, trimmed well aft—every rope drawing as tight as a fiddle string—causing the sea to boil like soapsuds under our bows as we fairly flew through the water."[138]

Seminole was gaining on *Fox*, still about three miles off. Mackie and his shipmates were finally able to get a clear view of their quarry, a long, low side-wheel steamer with masts and funnels swept back at a "fearful rake." *Fox* was painted a very light gray color all over, the better to blend in with the haze.

Seminole opened fire, first with her thirty-pounder Parrott rifle and then with her largest artillery piece, an eleven-inch smoothbore gun. A shell from the latter burst just under *Fox*'s bow, sending up a deluge of spray but causing no other damage. Again *Fox* altered course, this time to port, and ran boldly right across *Seminole*'s bow, a mile and a half ahead of the warship.

Seminole altered course as well, and now the two ships were running on parallel courses about a mile apart, their bows pointing northwest and

both still heading in for the beach. Captain
Clary ordered all the guns that would bear
to begin firing, with special instructions to
try and strike *Fox*'s wheelhouse. "Sink her if
you can," Clary ordered.[139]

Just as *Fox* was about to enter the
breakers on the Bolivar shore, Adkins put
up his helm and made a sharp, ninety-
degree turn to port. Now *Fox* had her bow
pointed to the southwest, running along
the shore in water too shallow for most of
the blockaders to get near. At that moment,
the leadsman near *Seminole*'s bow called out
the sounding—"by the deep three fathoms
[eighteen feet]"—and *Seminole* drew sixteen
feet. Clary ordered a hard turn to port as
well and continued running alongside *Fox*,
on courses parallel to the shore.

Marine sergeant John Freeman
Mackie, who witnessed the chase
of *Fox* and wrote about it many
years later. *Naval History and
Heritage Command.*

By this time, the other blockading ships
were approaching, belching coal smoke and firing wildly at the low, gray
runner. Sergeant Mackie later recalled the remarkable scene:

> Penguin *and the* Ossipee, *with all the other vessels of the fleet, had
> joined us, and opened fire upon her, with no better success than ourselves, all
> shots flying wide of the mark. The most tremendous excitement prevailed
> on board each vessel. Captain Clary raved and stamped about in an intense
> but subdued tone, swore like a pirate, and directed in as cool a manner as
> if we were having a race for a purse, but all to no effect. Shot after shot
> went over her and exploded on the beach beyond. Some exploded short of the
> steamer and covered her with spray; some in the air over her deck; others cut
> the water just ahead of her; one just grazed her stern, but not one touched
> her so far as we could see.*[140]*

Mackie also observed Captain Adkins, recalling that he "for the last
hour had been walking the bridge between the wheel houses, both hands
in the pockets of his pea jacket, smoking a cigar as unconcernedly as if
there was nothing going on…He never flinched an inch or changed his
manner, but kept quietly on, directing his ship as if it were an every-
day affair."[141]

"Shot, shell, grape, shrapnell [sic], every missile which the ingenuity of Satan and his children, the Yankees, have invented was thrown at, around, over, and in the waters beneath the doomed victim," according to a newspaper account published soon after.[142] Only four of those shots actually struck the runner, and none did enough damage to stop or even slow her. One by one, *Fox*'s pursuers dropped astern or were forced to sheer off into deeper water while Harry Wachsen guided the runner through the narrow Northeast Channel. *Seminole* was the last to break off the chase, firing a single eleven-inch shell toward *Fox* as she passed out of range. According to Mackie, Simpson Adkins responded by hoisting a Confederate flag at *Fox*'s stern, which he then "dipped" (ran up and down quickly) three times as a salute to his pursuers.[143]

During the latter part of the war, the Confederate government in Richmond began to recognize that reliance on private blockade runners was not providing sufficient imports of munitions, raw materials and other essentials to maintaining the war effort. This was partly addressed in March 1864, when the Confederate congress passed a law obligating blockade runners to allot half their cargoes, both in- and outbound, to material being shipped on behalf of the Confederate government. But still it wasn't enough—the profits to be made on civilian goods, particularly on upscale items like silks, preserved fruits and coffee, was just too great to be abandoned. Eventually the Confederacy equipped its own small fleet of blockade runners, government-owned ships commanded by officers of the Confederate navy. One of these, *Owl*, was a 446-ton steel-hulled paddle steamer built at Liverpool in 1864. *Owl* ran the blockade into Galveston just once, in mid-April 1865. Although no one in Galveston yet knew it, Robert E. Lee's Army of Northern Virginia had already laid down its arms at Appomattox Court House.

Owl's commander was John Newland Maffitt, one of the best known of all Confederate naval officers. In 1861, after serving nearly thirty years in the U.S. Navy, Maffitt resigned his commission and entered Confederate service. Maffitt is best known for his command of the commerce raider *Florida*, which in a single cruise destroyed or captured forty-seven U.S. merchantmen. Maffitt was an aggressive officer. A reporter for the *New York World* who encountered Maffitt in neutral Havana wrote, "Captain Maffitt is no ordinary character. He is vigorous, energetic, bold, quick and dashing, and the sooner he is caught and hung the better it will be."[144]

On the evening of April 14, 1865, Maffitt tried to bring *Owl* into Galveston by the same route Sim Adkins and Harry Wachsen had used with *Fox*, by

A Confederate lookout tower on the Bolivar shore, opposite Galveston. An observer here could signal runners offshore or summon assistance. *Library of Congress.*

way of the Northeast Channel off Bolivar Peninsula. Maffitt's navigation was off, though, and the big, pink-painted runner grounded on Bird Key, a shoal several hundred yards off the beach.[145] Maffitt tried running his wheels forward and back to get off the sand, to no avail. Eventually Maffitt managed to communicate his situation to a lookout station on shore, which in turn was able to pass word on to Galveston. From there, the converted civilian riverboat *Diana* crossed the entrance to Galveston Bay, located the stranded steamer and succeeded in hauling *Owl* off the shoal.

Maffitt himself presented an odd picture:

> *Upon arriving alongside, all were anxiously looking to see Capt. Maffitt, who was standing in the gangway of his ship to receive us, but none could recognize him, as we expected to find him fixed up with gold lace &c., but it was not so. He looked more like a cool, unconcerned passenger than a Captain in the C.S. Navy, with a Scotch cap, a torn coat, and a pair of rubber shoes, without socks. This was the condition in which we found him, but any sailor knows full well how to meet another. He was glad to meet us.*[146]

No doubt Maffitt was glad to see help arrive. It was a near-run thing, but by dawn, both ships had successfully withdrawn into the safety of Galveston Harbor, apparently without the Federals ever realizing Maffitt's ship was there. The *Galveston Daily News* later reported the incident, praising Maffitt's cool demeanor in that situation. "How like a sailor and a man," the *News* wrote, "did he stand by his ship, the *Owl*, when, in the hour of peril, within reach of Yankee guns, and had they known his situation, could have captured ship and crew."[147]

Owl's near-disastrous grounding on Bird Key has an unfortunate postscript for historians. The story was told at the time in the *Galveston Daily News*, but decades later, in 1901, an anonymous editor would dig it out of the files and rewrite it, this time with the added embellishment that the entire thing happened in broad daylight, with Maffitt braving a torrent of Yankee gunfire to bring his runner into Galveston, cheered on by thousands of citizens lining the wharves and rooftops of the city. Maffitt's widow reprinted this embellished version in a biography of her late husband, published in 1906, effectively giving it her personal imprimatur. Emma Maffitt's dramatic tale of Yankee gunboats "raining shot and shell around the stranded vessel"[148] has now been taken as unchallenged fact for more than a century, but that's not the way it happened.

Chapter 9

COLLAPSE

We had not been acting very honorably for the past two days, but after all we were only taking our own.
—Private Z. T. Winfree, Second Texas Infantry

Around mid-morning on Monday, June 5, 1865, a small side-wheel steamer rounded the fishhook at the eastern end of Galveston Island, maneuvered cautiously around the pilings placed to block the entrance to Galveston Harbor and moved slowly up the channel, coming to a stop a few yards off Central Wharf along the waterfront. Heaving lines flew across the gap between the ship and the wharf. The ship had the unmistakable look of a runner—the low, narrow hull and haze-gray paint streaked with rust and salt. Her superstructure was cut down to reduce her silhouette. Two light-colored funnels, one forward of the paddlewheel boxes and one aft, completed her shape, one that had become so familiar to those on the Galveston waterfront over the previous few months.

But *Cornubia* was not a runner (not anymore, anyway); she was a Union gunboat. She had begun her life as a British coastal steamer, was converted to blockade running in 1862 and, in the next year, made nine successful round voyages into Wilmington, North Carolina. Her luck ran out in November 1863 when she was captured by the Union gunboats *James Adger* and *Niphon*. The U.S. Navy purchased her and sent her out on the blockade, where she cruised in search of her former sisters; the poacher had been made gamekeeper. Now she flew the Stars and Stripes at her main gaff,

Central Wharf, Galveston, as seen in 1861 from atop Hendley's Row. *Rosenberg Library.*

and on this June morning, she also displayed a blue-and-white pennant, signifying the presence on board of Captain Benjamin Franklin Sands, commanding the Third Division of the West Gulf Blockading Squadron. It was nearly the end.[149]

***

In the summer of 1863, when Confederate general Henry McCullough decreed that "the city of Galveston and vicinity are entrenched camps,"[150] Galveston was already becoming a desolate place. Many Galvestonians who could afford to move their households inland had done so after *South Carolina*'s bombardment of the city two years before; many more left during the pell-mell evacuation of the city ahead of Union occupation in October 1862. Just about every civilian who could leave did so unless compelled to stay by poverty or, for a few, the demands of business. While successful merchants like Thomas W. House maintained residences in Galveston and accumulated substantial fortunes running cotton and goods through the blockade, for most in the city, the last two years of the war were an increasingly grim struggle to get by.[151]

Galveston remained under threat of invasion long after the island's recapture by Magruder in January 1863, and during the latter stages of the war, there were more soldiers stationed on the island than there were civilians. Crimes, both petty and violent, became commonplace. Houses left vacant by evacuated civilians were stripped of their furnishings, and fences and outbuildings were torn down for firewood. Bored soldiers found or created various forms of entertainment to amuse themselves, as soldiers throughout history have. Vice flourished despite the Confederate provost marshal's efforts to eradicate it. Soldiers convicted of different offenses were assigned creative punishments like wearing a ball and chain or marching up and down Market Street wearing a barrel inscribed with the word "THIEF," but these penalties did little to curb the problem.[152]

Texas as a whole never lacked for sufficient provender during the war, but hunger became an increasing problem in Galveston during the conflict. The combined effects of the blockade and the shortage of manpower and transport combined to cause serious logistical obstacles in keeping people properly fed. What food could be acquired was often of very poor quality and prohibitively expensive. Soldiers and civilians suffered alike. For one company of the Eighth Texas Infantry, garrisoned at Galveston, frustration boiled over on the last Sunday of February 1864, when the soldiers were issued as rations the carcass of a scrawny, sickly steer they deemed entirely inedible. Instead of cutting up the beef and distributing it to individual messes, the soldiers turned out at 9:30 a.m. with their rifles and organized a formal funeral cortege. The soldiers put the rejected beef on a stick and paraded it through the town in grand funereal style, under reversed arms and to the accompaniment of muffled drums. When they reached the public square in front of the courthouse, they held a mock funeral and buried it, reading a formal eulogy over the remains.[153] One soldier who participated later explained his and his messmates' actions in a letter to a Houston newspaper:

> *The movement was not dictated by any spirit of mutiny, far from it. The beef which had been issued to the Regiment for several days previous had been condemned by a Board of Survey, and pronounced unfit for use... Their resolution had been taken not to receive the beef, and the burial of it was simply intended as a protest against the insult offered in persisting in sending meat, which every one, who would take the trouble to examine, could see was totally unfit to eat.*[154]

Civilians went without as well. Several weeks after the soldiers eulogized their rancid steer carcass on the courthouse square, the Confederate officer commanding at Galveston, Brigadier General James Hawes, responded to a shortage of milled flour by ordering the military commissary to stop selling the staple to soldiers' families. Hawes was a fractious and self-important officer who had already been shuffled around various combat commands during the first part of the war; even Braxton Bragg, an infamously disputatious man in his own right, couldn't stand him. In mid-April 1864, Hawes found himself put in charge of the defenses at Galveston. When Hawes cut off the provision of flour to soldiers' families, women began protesting outside both his residence and his headquarters in the customs house. Ralph J. Smith, a veteran soldier in the Second Texas Infantry who helped disperse the women at the general's quarters, recalled that "no one who has not seen a mob of this kind clamoring for bread can have any conception of the crazed and uncontrollable rage of the participants or appreciate the difficulty of quieting them without the shedding of blood." Hawes had the provost guard arrest the women and put several he deemed to be ringleaders on the next train to Houston with orders not to return. This act, along with other perceived high-handed deeds by Hawes, earned the general the sobriquet "Beast Butler of Galveston."[155]

Morale problems in units stationed on the island became severe. Hawes was replaced as commanding officer at Galveston in April 1865 by Colonel Ashbel Smith, who before the war had been a highly regarded local physician. Smith was a popular and practical choice, but there was little even he could do at that point. Desertions had become commonplace, and there were several serious instances of units mutinying. By the latter part of April, news of Lee's surrender at Appomattox Court House and Lincoln's assassination had reached Texas, and it became clear to all concerned that the end was near. On May 14, Colonel Smith learned of an attempt by several hundred men of his regiment to desert en masse. He and an armed guard met the would-be deserters at the foot of the railroad trestle leading to the mainland. Remarkably, by reassurance, appeals to their remaining sense of duty and the force of his own personality, Smith was able to convince them to return to their quarters.[156]

The runners knew it was near the end, too. Just two steamships from Havana successfully made the dash into Galveston through the Yankee blockade in May 1865: *Wren*, around May 5, and her sister *Lark* on May 24.[157]

On the same night that *Lark* got into Galveston successfully, *Denbigh* grounded on Bird Key in about the same spot where John Newland Maffitt

The U.S. Customs House in Galveston was rushed to completion before Texas seceded in 1861. As the first structure built by the federal government in Texas, both sides saw it as a symbol of U.S. authority in Galveston and the state. *Author's photo.*

had run *Owl* ashore a few weeks previously. This time, though, there was no one to assist, and the iron-hulled paddle steamer was still there the next morning when the sun came up. Her crew took to the boats and pulled frantically for the Bolivar shore while Union gunboats *Cornubia* and *Princess Royal* opened fire. A boat's crew from USS *Seminole* boarded the wreck, gathered up the ship's papers and set *Denbigh* ablaze. They probably got into some liquor found on board as well because one seaman from *Seminole*, Luke Robins, accidentally set off his own weapon while clambering back into the boat, killing himself instantly. Two other men were found to be drunk by the time they got back to *Seminole* and were put in irons. The entire episode was over by 7:00 a.m.[158] In all, *Denbigh* had made seven round voyages between Havana and Mobile and six between Havana and Galveston, the second-best confirmed record of any runner in the conflict.[159] Years later, William Watson wrote of her:

> One of the most successful, and certainly one of the most profitable, steamers that sailed out of Havana to the Confederate States was a somewhat old, and by no means a fast, steamer named the Denbigh...She was small

in size, and not high above water, and painted in such a way as not to be readily seen at a distance. She was light on coal, made but little smoke, and depended more upon strategy than speed. She carried large cargoes of cotton, and it was generally allowed that the little Denbigh *was a more profitable boat than any of the larger and swifter cracks.*[160]

At around three o'clock that same morning, while *Denbigh*'s crew was struggling in vain to get their ship afloat before the sunrise revealed their location to the Federal fleet, the runner *Lark* slipped into the harbor. *Lark*'s master noticed that the batteries at Fort Point appeared to be deserted. He continued into the harbor and tied up at Central Wharf as usual. Soon he found his vessel surrounded by perhaps two hundred armed soldiers, who went on board in search of liquor. One soldier who witnessed the event later recalled that "they swarmed all through the vessel like bees." Some soldiers initially held back, expecting Colonel Smith to come riding up with the provost guard, but that didn't happen. "The soldiers became 'enthused,' and called for everybody in sight to come up. Everybody 'came,' and now the pillage became general. The *Lark* was loaded with army and hospital supplies for the Confederacy. Soldiers, citizens, women and children came aboard and helped themselves." *Lark*'s skipper managed to herd everyone off the ship long enough to cast off from the wharf and move the runner out into the harbor, but the looters took to rowboats and again swarmed the steamer. The pillaging went on into the afternoon; there had been a complete breakdown of both military discipline and civilian law and order. The soldier who witnessed the looting of *Lark* was regretful but not apologetic: "We had not been acting very honorably for the past two days, but after all we were only taking our own." That same evening, *Lark* got under way, without waiting for an outbound cargo. Coming alongside the wharf again just long enough to take on board *Denbigh*'s crew, who had been ferried across the entrance to the bay from the Bolivar Peninsula, *Lark* steamed up the channel and around the harbor obstructions and dashed out again into the Gulf of Mexico, bound for Havana. With both her own and *Denbigh*'s crew aboard, *Lark* became the last steamship to clear a Confederate port.[161]

The looters who swarmed over *Lark* at Central Wharf on May 24 didn't know it, but that same morning General Magruder, commanding the Confederate District of Texas, addressed a letter to Captain Sands off Galveston, asking Sands to convey Colonel Ashbel Smith and a prominent Galveston attorney, William Pitt Ballinger, to New Orleans to begin negotiating an armistice between Union and Confederate forces in

Above: USS *Fort Jackson*, flagship of the Third Division of the West Gulf Blockading Squadron. It was on this ship, anchored off Galveston, that the Confederate Trans-Mississippi Department surrendered on June 2, 1865. *Library of Congress.*

Left: Captain Benjamin Franklin Sands, seen here in a postwar photo, raised the flag over the U.S. Customs House in Galveston and described it as "the closing act of the great rebellion." *Library of Congress.*

Texas. The state's governor, Pendleton Murrah, concurred in the request. General E. Kirby Smith, commanding the Confederate Trans-Mississippi Department, was initially astounded to read dispatches from his subordinate Magruder in which Prince John explained that he had "lost control" of his command. Nonetheless, Smith quickly came to understand the reality that his military command was one that existed only on paper.[162]

Late on the afternoon of Friday, June 2, 1865, Generals Smith and Magruder boarded Sands's flagship, USS *Fort Jackson*, anchored off Galveston. U.S. brigadier general Edmund J. Davis, a lawyer from Laredo who had opposed secession and eventually cast his lot with the Union, was present to represent Federal forces. At 5:00 p.m., in Captain Sands's cabin, these men signed the document surrendering the Trans-Mississippi Department, the last major Confederate command to yield to the Union. The American Civil War was over.[163]

Three days later, after allowing sufficient time for word of the surrender to be passed to the few Confederate forces remaining in their defensive works up and down the coast, Sands boarded the light-draft *Cornubia* and, with USS *Preston* trailing behind, entered Galveston Harbor. Sands disembarked with a handful of naval officers—but no armed escort—and was met on the wharf by a Confederate officer, who accompanied them to the mayor's office above the old city market, just one block from Hendley's Row and the old JOLO watch tower. There, the mayor and Sands both briefly addressed a crowd of soldiers and civilians "who had assembled in considerable numbers." Both men made assurances of their goodwill and urged the population to go about their business peaceably. Sands told the crowd that he carried a sidearm that day not out of any fear for his own safety but as a sign of respect for the mayor and local officials. Then, along with the mayor, Sands continued on to the old U.S. Customs House, where he "hoisted our flag, which now, at last, was flying over every foot of our territory, this being the closing act of the great rebellion."[164]

Epilogue
REDISCOVERY

Full fathom five thy father lies;
Of his bones are coral made;
Those are pearls that were his eyes;
Nothing of him that doth fade,
But doth suffer a sea-change
Into something rich and strange.
–Shakespeare, The Tempest

On June 23, 1865 the new U.S. president, Andrew Johnson, issued an executive order formally lifting the blockade at "all the ports aforesaid, including that of Galveston and other ports west of the Mississippi River," effective July 1. Galveston was the only southern port mentioned by name in Johnson's order.[165]

In the months, years and decades after the close of the war, the excitement and emphasis on blockade running over the previous four years gave way to a focus on rebuilding commerce and trade. Some of the cash fortunes that had been made running cotton out of the state under the noses of Admiral Farragut's squadron evaporated with the collapse of the Confederacy, although shrewd businessmen like William Marsh Rice and Thomas W. House remained well positioned to continue building their mercantile empires after the war. Texas had not much suffered the ravages of large-scale fighting or Union occupation and was poised to embark on a new boom of economic development through immigration, railroad building and expanded settlements in the state's frontier areas.

Up and down the Texas coast, the burned and sunken remains of blockade-running vessels slowly succumbed to the elements. Those that had been salvaged at the time of their loss were again picked over for anything useful or valuable. Wood dried out, cracked and rotted, and iron elements rusted and fell apart, buffeted by surf and occasional storms. Locals told stories about the wrecks, but the details of their histories, circumstances of their loss and even their names gradually passed from living memory.

***

The first Civil War blockade runner to be identified and explored in modern times in Texas was the wreck of *Acadia*, several hundred yards off the beach, between San Luis Pass and the mouth of the Brazos River. The wreck, in shallow water, remained visible over the decades, with one of the ship's funnels reportedly extending above the water for almost a century. *Acadia* was a well-known local landmark, but despite its familiarity to locals, the wreck remained undisturbed for a century, due in part to difficult diving conditions at the site and lack of easy access to that part of the shore.

In the 1960s a Houston dentist, Wendell Eldredge Pierce, took an interest in the site and began diving on it. Pierce was an experienced scuba diver and longtime treasure hunter who had recovered material from wrecks both in the United States and the Caribbean. On the *Acadia* site, Pierce sometimes brought along a friend, but he usually worked alone and sometimes at night. Given the generally poor visibility in the water, the state of the surf was of more concern to Pierce than lighting conditions. Pierce would watch the weather closely and head for the site when conditions seemed calm enough for diving. Sometimes he would take a break in the middle of the day, leaving his scuba tanks tied off to the wreck while he napped in the shade of his vehicle on the beach.[166]

Given that Pierce was a one-man operation, working without specialized equipment or tools, he seems to have done a reasonable job of sorting out the various elements of the wreck in his own mind. He identified what he believed were the bow and stern of the vessel and determined that the bow was oriented toward the beach. He located and tentatively identified large features of the wreck that he interpreted as a boiler and a water tank, as well as firebricks from the furnace. He recorded that the surviving parts of the ship's wooden hull were still sheathed with brass, although he probably meant Muntz metal, a copper-based alloy commonly used in the nineteenth century to protect hull timbers from the wood-boring teredo worm.

Regrettably, Pierce died suddenly in October 1973 after suffering an apparent heart attack at the age of fifty-one. He left behind hundreds of artifacts that he had recovered from the *Acadia* site, including earthenware jars and glass bottles, tools, lamps, assorted machinery fittings, cases of door and window hardware and an intact example of an early flushing toilet. Two years before, Pierce had been obligated to obtain a permit from the Texas Antiquities Committee (now the Texas Historical Commission) to comply with the Texas Antiquities Code, passed in 1969. Because Pierce was a private citizen without the resources to conserve the artifacts, which, under the Antiquities Code, were considered state property, the Houston Museum of Natural Science took out the permit under its auspices and became the initial repository for the material. Frank Hole, a faculty member at Rice University, agreed to serve as archaeologist for the collection, although very few, if any, artifacts were recovered from the *Acadia* site after that time by Pierce. Hole placed some of the iron objects Pierce had recovered in electrolysis, a slow process that helps remove some of the damaging salts and minerals that leach into ferrous (iron-based) metal after long immersion in seawater. He also hired a student to begin the yearlong process of cleaning the other artifacts. Hole then left the United States to work on an extended archaeological project in the Middle East.

When he returned in the autumn of 1973, Hole learned of Pierce's recent death. He also finally had time to go through the *Acadia* material recovered by Pierce in detail. He discovered that the dentist had attempted to clean or restore many of the artifacts in ways that damaged them. Pierce broke apart encrustations, in some cases damaging or destroying the artifacts inside. He had rinsed iron artifacts and then coated them with hot wax, sealing damaging chlorides inside. Pierce had used harsh methods, including acid, to clean some artifacts, and some others he tried to restore by filling gaps with pink dental cement.

More important archaeologically, though, was the lack of detailed records. Pierce left behind scattered notes documenting his trips to the site and the work he did with artifacts, but they were incomplete. Pierce himself was gone, and because he had mostly worked alone, there was no way to clarify or expand on what he had written. While Pierce had often noted what part of the ship he was working in—as he had come to understand it, by years spent groping around in the turbid green water—he apparently never drew a detailed plan of the site and was unable to document exactly where artifacts were found. While Pierce ended up with a large collection of materials that hint at the range of fittings and cargo aboard blockade runners like *Acadia*, the lack of documentation to understand them in the context of the site itself represents a tremendous lost opportunity for a deeper understanding of the ship. Frank Hole compiled a report and artifact analysis based on Pierce's collection of *Acadia* artifacts. The collection itself now resides at the Brazoria County Historical Museum in Angleton, Texas, where its materials are often featured in exhibitions and are available for study by researchers.

***

The circumstances of *Denbigh's* discovery in 1996 have been described previously in the Acknowledgements. Barto Arnold, who had served for two decades as the state marine archaeologist in Austin, had recently assumed a position at the Institute of Nautical Archaeology (INA), located on the main campus of Texas A&M University in College Station. Taking the role of principal investigator and project director, Arnold secured an antiquities permit from the state to investigate the site and was able to bring the newly christened *Denbigh* Project under the aegis of INA, a move that opened doors for much wider public exposure than would have been possible otherwise, as well as better opportunities for funding.

Over the next eighteen months, Arnold, Tom Oertling and the author dug into extensive historical research on the ship and organized a series of two- and three-day dives on the site, working with volunteer groups like the Southwest Underwater Archaeological Society. On one occasion, a U.S. Navy Reserve Salvage Dive Unit used the *Denbigh* site for a drill weekend. Although these dives did not include excavation, they allowed the project team gradually to build up a clear picture of the site, parts of the wreck exposed above the sandy bottom and the likely outlines of the buried hull.

Denbigh lies some hundreds of yards off the beach at Bolivar Peninsula, not far from the entrance to Galveston Bay. The water there is shallow, and when the tide is very low, the upper part of the ship's large, box-like boiler is visible above the surface, flanked by the remains of the outer rims of the vessel's iron paddlewheels. The burned-out shell of the iron hull itself gradually settled into the sand, as wrecks on that part of the Texas coast typically do, until it encountered a denser layer of clay. In the case of *Denbigh*, that happened to be just about the depth of the ship's hull to the level of the main deck, so that the iron deck beams around the middle of the ship are almost exactly at the same level as the sandy bottom. Immediately aft of the boiler, a heavy axle stretched across the ship between the paddlewheels, with an assortment of cranks and flanges on it. The entire hull of the ship, or what's left of it, is buried.

Over four summers (1999–2002), the Institute of Nautical Archaeology held a series of two-month-long field projects on the *Denbigh* site each June and July. The field project each year included Arnold as PI/project director and Tom Oertling as co-PI/assistant director. (The author, also as co-PI, worked primarily in historical research, illustration and website development.) The field crews typically consisted of ten to fourteen undergraduate and graduate students, with a handful of non-student volunteers looking for an unusual diving and research experience. The project each year was based out of the Pelican Island campus of Texas A&M University at Galveston, where team members lived in the dorms. Crews set out each morning with the dive boats on trailers, hauled them across the entrance to Galveston Bay by way of a state highway department ferry, and launched them on the Bolivar Peninsula not far from the wreck site. Later in the project, teams sometimes launched the boats at the university's small boat harbor, about forty-five minutes from the *Denbigh* site by boat.

On most days, two boats traveled to the site. After arriving at the site and setting an anchor to account for the winds and current, the crew would divide into pairs, who worked as teams underwater. As part of their routines, the first team into the water would usually lay out the hoses for the induction dredges. These hoses used a continuous flow of water to draw loose sand and small shells away from points where the divers were excavating. (The outflow from the dredges was all run through mesh bags to capture any small artifacts that happened to get drawn up with the sand, but this proved to be a rare occurrence.) Visibility at the site was typical for the confluence of estuarial and seawater on the upper Texas coast, which is to say, *terrible*. Once the divers got to work, stirring up silt, sand and other bottom sediments, they spent most of their time working by feel alone. The first dive of each day in each excavation area was usually devoted to clearing away dense clumps of *Sargassum* (seaweed) and other debris that would collect in the dug-out depression overnight.

During the first summer field season in 1999, the crew focused on excavating an area forward of the midships boiler and engine assembly, where the forward cargo hold would have been. After gradually working down into the space over a period of several weeks, the crew reached the bottom of the hull to find almost nothing. Whatever inbound cargo had been there when the ship was lost had long since been destroyed or salvaged. Most of the ship's hull plating on the port side of the ship forward had been

Archaeologists diving at the *Denbigh* site, 2002. *Institute of Nautical Archaeology.*

broken down flat, a result of the combined effect of natural deterioration and periodic battering by storms.

The second field season, in 2000, shifted its focus to the after part of the vessel, where both another cargo hold and the cabins for officers and passengers would presumably have been. This area should have yielded a diversity of artifacts reflecting life aboard the steamship, but as with the forward cargo hold, very little of what might have been there survived. The crew did find evidence of the fire that destroyed the ship, in the form of charred ceramics and small bits of melted glass, but very little that was recognizable.

In both 1999 and 2000, limited excavation was conducted amidships, mostly on the port side of the ship. One early excavation unit was just behind what the team believed was the bulkhead aft of the engine room. This particular unit revealed portions of the collapsed iron bulkhead, with a large quantity of coal underneath. This coal was interpreted as being part of an auxiliary bunker, fitted due to the necessity of the ship having to carry enough fuel for a complete round voyage between Havana and Galveston; obtaining a substantial quantity of coal in the blockaded Texas port would have been very difficult and perhaps impossible by 1865.

The last two field seasons, in the summers of 2001 and 2002, focused entirely on excavating the middle section of the ship, containing the boiler and engine, and the area just outside the hull around the portside paddlewheel. The area around the portside engine was dug out, as was the space directly in front of the boiler, where the firemen would have stoked the ship's four furnaces. Limited excavation had been conducted in those areas in 1999 and 2000, but in 2001, it became the primary focus of the fieldwork. Although the team had been disappointed in its efforts to document the ship's inbound cargo, this new focus on the central part of the hull enabled them to record that space in much more detail than might otherwise have been the case. The end result was a much more complete understanding of *Denbigh*'s hull construction and power plant than with any other blockade runner at that time. This data, accumulated bit by bit over the course of several hundred individual dives, enabled the team to make detailed internal reconstructions of that part of the ship, a substantial contribution to archaeologists' and historians' understanding of the technology used in blockade running.

The midships excavation did reveal some additional and unexpected hints at the ship's history and her crew. Perhaps the most important of these findings was that despite not being mentioned in the historical record, the burned-out hulk of the ship was clearly picked over by salvors some time after the Union boarding party burned her in May 1865. This became obvious when the archaeologists noted that many of the small, lightweight parts of the engine machinery had been tossed into a heap on the deck in the narrow space between the engines and the boiler furnaces. This loose refuse eventually concreted into a solid mass that prevented excavation down to the keel in that spot. The *Denbigh* Project team found itself working with the remains of a ship that had been shelled, burned and finally picked clean of everything that an unidentified group of salvors found useful in 1865.

Nonetheless, there were some surprises—artifacts that teased at a more complex story of the ship and her crew than can probably ever be known for sure. Among the artifacts found was the lower porcelain leg of a doll that originally would have had ceramic limbs and a head sewn onto a cloth body. A trace of the black paint on the doll's molded foot remained. Was it on board as a gift, purchased by a blockade-running crew member in Havana or Mobile for a beloved child at home? Or was it older, perhaps from *Denbigh*'s days as an excursion steamer on the Welsh coast?

Several very large artifacts were recovered during the field work on *Denbigh*, including part of the boiler's superheater, one of the two engines' connecting rods and one of the mechanisms that "feathered" the blades of the paddlewheel as it turned, making it more efficient. Notwithstanding the artifacts, much of the great contribution made by the *Denbigh* Project was accomplished not during the fieldwork in 1999–2002 but in the archival research and writing that has come since. This process began in 2001 with Arnold's reissue of William Watson's long-overlooked *The Adventures of a Blockade Runner*, the best and most comprehensive first-person account of blockade running under sail. In the years since, Arnold has published numerous works, including a reprinting of the late W.T. Block's *Schooner Sail to Starboard* and separate volumes of blockade-runner prize court proceedings and *Denbigh's* civilian cargo manifests. These reprinted narratives get "down into the weeds," as Arnold says, and yield detailed glimpses into daily life of specific people in addition to the day-to-day processes of the blockade-running trade. Arnold argues that "one needs to get steeped in the minutiae to achieve deep understanding."[167] Between four summers of field excavation and the ongoing intensive archival research that has followed it, *Denbigh* is now almost certainly the most thoroughly researched and documented blockade runner of the American Civil War, as well as one of the best-documented shipwrecks of any type in North America.

***

In the late 1970s, a group of sport divers in the Galveston area set out to find the wreck of *Will o' the Wisp*. They spent more than two years exhaustively pouring over contemporary accounts of the ship and her destruction. By early 1982, they had zeroed in on a site off the beach, near the western end of the city. "I finally felt I knew where the ship was," a member of the team later recalled. "It wasn't one specific thing, but a whole lot of facts—going through newspapers, personal diaries, official records of the Union and Confederate navies, and particularly local newspapers."[168]

Working through the local county historical commission, by the summer of 1982, the group had secured a permit from the Texas Antiquities Committee to study the site. For a variety of logistical reasons, it proved impossible to arrange a magnetometer survey of the area until the fall of 1983, after Hurricane Alicia passed through the area. A magnetometer is a device that records fluctuations in the earth's magnetic field; by running one in a regular pattern back and forth across an area, it's possible to pinpoint the location of large quantities of ferrous metal. *Will o' the Wisp*, being over two hundred feet long and built of steel, should have been an easy target to find. And in fact, the team found something only a few hundred yards from the spot it had plotted.

Antiquities Committee archaeologist Mark Denton, who made the first dive on the site, immediately bruised his leg on a large iron bar sticking up from the sand that he'd been unable see in the turbid water.[169]

On subsequent trips to the site, divers located what they identified as arms (spokes) of the ship's paddlewheels and other features that seemed to verify the wreck's identity as *Will o' the Wisp*. "We can't say 100 percent that it is [*Wisp*]," one team member said. "All the evidence we have, historical evidence as to the [location of] the wreck site and what we've been able to see of the wreck so far, seems to say that it is." The team was careful not to describe the site's location in detail and stressed that the wreck, lying in state waters, was a protected archaeological site.[170]

The divers' project had the support of the county history museum, and through the winter of 1983–84, plans were being made to conduct further dives at the site. Later in 1984, though, Galveston County closed the museum and contracted its operation out to another local historical organization, and there the project stalled. No further studies of the wreck originally identified as *Will o' the Wisp* are known to have been completed.

More than two decades later, in September 2008, Hurricane Ike made landfall on Galveston Island, bringing with it a fourteen-foot storm surge that flooded about three-fourths of the island's homes and businesses. The storm surge was even higher farther north, on the Bolivar Peninsula, where the counter-clockwise motion of the storm winds swept many areas completely bare. A half dozen people died in Galveston, and at least ten more on the peninsula.[171]

As part of recovery efforts after the storm, the Texas General Land Office and the U.S. Army Corps of Engineers issued contracts to marine construction and salvage companies to make a survey of storm-damaged areas—both inland bays and in shallow water close to shore—to identify and remove any hurricane wreckage that might prove to be a hazard to navigation. As part of this process, one survey company located a previously unrecorded shipwreck a few hundred yards off the beach on Galveston Island, near the midpoint of the island. Side-scan sonar images of the site showed what was definitively a ship's hull, with a long, narrow spindle shape and a jumble of machinery amidships. The ship, whatever it might prove to be, was a large one—between 200 and 220 feet long.

In the summer of 2009, the Texas State Marine archaeologist, Steve Hoyt, acquired an antiquities permit and organized a series of dives at the site to see if it might be identified. Assisting Hoyt were several of the Texas Historical Commission's volunteer marine archaeological stewards,

The author (left) and Amy Borgens at the site of the second shipwreck identified as *Will o' the Wisp*, 2009. *Texas Historical Commission.*

including Gary McKee, John Luce, Doug Nowell, Craig Hlavinka and the author, along with Amy Borgens, a marine archaeologist working at the time with a commercial cultural resources management firm.

The wreck proved to be the remains of a metal-built side-wheel steamer, with roughly the bottom third of the hull intact. The ship had been extensively salvaged, but the paddlewheel shafts remained, dislodged and torqued into odd angles by the force used to wrench the engines out of the hull. Forward and aft of the space where the engines had been were two pairs of boilers, each with two furnaces. As with the other sites, visibility was extremely poor, but one thing Borgens noted immediately by touch was that the ship's hull plates and framing seemed extremely lightweight for a ship of that size, with the frames farther apart than usual. On a separate dive, two stewards succeeded in running a measuring tape from the bulkhead at the aft end of the machinery space to that at the forward end, a distance encompassing both pairs of boilers and the engine space between them. Their measurement was fifty-eight feet, almost a perfect match for the fifty-six-foot distance shown on tracings of the original *Wisp* builder's plan done more than forty years before by the Smithsonian Institution's William Geoghagen.

Twenty-five years before, the team that identified the earlier site as *Will o' the Wisp* had explained that "it wasn't one specific thing, but a whole lot of facts" that led them to conclude that that wreck was the famous blockade runner. That's often how shipwrecks are identified, but now that same process points to the site discovered after Hurricane Ike as being *Will o' the Wisp*. There are multiple points of congruence beyond the length of the engine space. The size of the wreck overall—a little over two hundred feet long and about one-tenth as wide—is about right for the Clyde-built blockade runner. There is also the very lightweight, widely spaced framing that Borgens noticed on her first dive, which recalls Tom Taylor's description of *Wisp* as "shamefully put together, and most fragile." Taylor had also noted in his book that *Will o' the Wisp* was fitted with four tubular boilers, encompassing between them eight furnaces, the same as on the wreck documented in 2009. Finally, the new wreck's location is a better fit for contemporary newspaper accounts of the ship's loss and subsequent salvage in 1865 than the site located in the early 1980s.

For now, the second site seems to be a much more likely candidate for *Will o' the Wisp*. More work needs to be done to document the site, and hopefully this work will generate new data that will definitively confirm or refute the identification proposed here. The previous site identified as *Wisp* should probably be re-designated as an unidentified wreck; more work needs to be done there, as well, to see if that site matches some other vessel known to have been lost in the area.

All the shipwreck sites described in this chapter lie in Texas state waters and, as pre–twentieth century sites, are protected State Antiquities Landmarks. They should not be disturbed.

***

The work of archaeologists, historians and others on the shipwrecks described in this epilogue underscores the ongoing interest in the legacy of blockade running on the Texas coast during the Civil War. It's a story that, while set far from the center of the conflict and often eclipsed by the better-known tales of Charleston and Cape Fear, nonetheless remains central to the course of the war in the Trans-Mississippi Theater. Galveston and Texas were destined to be the final outposts of the Confederacy, and their surrender in June 1865 truly represented, as Captain Sands observed, "the closing act of the great rebellion." The struggle between the runners and the blockaders on the Texas coast encapsulates many of the broad themes of the larger war, with the South—brash, daring and overconfident to the point of arrogance—achieving success early on against a foe unprepared for the task at hand. But over time, hard-worn experience, material resources and dogged determination gradually gave Northern forces an increasing advantage, to the point at which victory, though long delayed, became inevitable. It is a remarkable story of men, ships, cotton and cash that continues to resonate across the decades.

NOTES

CHAPTER 1

1. D.W. Meinig, *Imperial Texas: An Interpretive Essay in Cultural Geography* (Austin: University of Texas Press, 1969), 26–27; Keith Guthrie, *Texas Forgotten Ports: Mid-Gulf Coast Ports from Corpus Christi to Matagorda Bay* (Austin, TX: Eakin Press, 1988), 6–10.
2. Meinig, *Imperial Texas*, 28–29.
3. Randolph B. Campbell, *An Empire for Slavery: The Peculiar Institution in Texas, 1821–1865* (Baton Rouge: Louisiana State University, 1991), 253; Historical Census Browser, University of Virginia, http://mapserver.lib. virginia.edu/php/start.php?year=V1860.
4. Charles Waldo Hayes, *History of the Island and City of Galveston* (Austin, TX: Jenkins Garrett Press, 1974), 749–51.

CHAPTER 2

5. Craig L. Symonds, *Lincoln and His Admirals* (New York: Oxford, 2008), 40–41.
6. Abraham Lincoln, "Proclamation 81—Declaring a Blockade of Ports in Rebellious States," April 19, 1861. Online by Gerhard Peters and John

T. Woolley, the American Presidency Project. www.presidency.ucsb.edu/ws/?pid=70101.

7. Donald A. Petrie, *The Prize Game: Lawful Looting on the High Seas in the Days of Fighting Sail* (New York: Berkley, 1999), 106.

8. Symonds, *Lincoln and His Admirals*, 39.

9. Symonds, *Lincoln and His Admirals*, 39; David Herbert Donald, *Lincoln* (New York: Touchstone, 1996), 302. Just over a century later, in 1962, the Kennedy administration faced a similar dilemma over the importation of Soviet missiles into Cuba. Recognizing that there was no precedent for imposing a blockade or stopping Soviet ships at sea without it being seen as an act of war, Kennedy was careful in his language, declaring a "quarantine" of Cuba, rather than a blockade.

10. Amanda Foreman, *A World on Fire: Britain's Crucial Role in the American Civil War* (New York: Random House, 2010), 69.

11. Symonds, *Lincoln and His Admirals*, 39–40; Foreman, *World on Fire*, 69–70.

12. *Galveston Civilian and Gazette Weekly*, June 11, 1861, 1; *Beaumont Banner*, May 21, 1861, 2.

13. *Galveston Civilian and Gazette Weekly*, May 28, 1861, 2; James M. Schmidt, *Galveston and the Civil War: An Island City on the Maelstrom* (Charleston: The History Press, 2012), 32.

14. Paul H. Silverstone, *Warships of the Civil War Navies* (Annapolis, MD: Naval Institute Press, 1989), 80–81.

15. *Galveston Civilian and Gazette Weekly*, July 9, 1861, 1.

16. Ibid.

17. *Clarksville [Texas] Standard*, August 3, 1861, 1.

18. James Alden, "List of Vessels Captured by the USS *South Carolina*, off Galveston, from July 4 to July 7, 1861, Inclusive," *Official Records of the Union and Confederate Navies in the War of the Rebellion*, Series I, Vol. 16 (Washington, D.C., 1903), 575 (hereafter cited as ORN); ORN I:16, 578.

19. ORN I:16, 607–08; Schmidt, *Galveston and the Civil War*, 34.

20. Hayes, *History of the Island and City*, 498.

21. ORN I:16, 606–07.

22. Hayes, *History of the Island and City*, 498–99.

Chapter 3

23. W.T. Block, *Schooner Sail to Starboard: The U.S. Navy vs. Blockade Runners in the Western Gulf of Mexico* (College Station, TX: Institute of Nautical Archaeology, 2007), 42–43; ORN I:16, 665–66; David Dixon Porter, *The Naval History of the Civil War* (Secaucus, NJ: Castle, 1984), 841. Alden deemed *Soledad Cos* too small to attempt the long voyage to a prize court, so he sent her cargo on another vessel and retained the schooner as a tender. *Soledad Cos* was wrecked near Sabine Pass in late 1861 and her nine Union crew members taken prisoner. ORN I:17, 33.

24. ORN I:18, 104–06.

25. ORN I:19, 169.

26. William Watson, *Life in the Confederate Army: Being the Observations and Experiences of an Alien in the South During the American Civil War* (Baton Rouge: Louisiana State University, 1995), 2–3, 8–9.

27. William Watson, *The Adventures of a Blockade Runner; or, Trade in Time of War* (London: T. Fisher Unwin, 1893), 5–6.

28. Ibid., 13–14.

29. William Watson and J. Barto Arnold III, *The Civil War Adventures of a Blockade Runner* (College Station: Texas A&M University, 2001).

30. ORN I:21, 295.

31. Ibid., 293–95; Block, *Schooner Sail to Starboard*, 123–24.

32. Marcus W. Price, "Ships That Tested the Blockade of the Gulf Ports, 1861–1865, Part IV," *American Neptune* (1952), 236.

Chapter 4

33. ORN I:16, 841; Confederate Citizens' file, "John H. Sterrett," Confederate Papers Relating to Citizens or Business Firms, RG 109 NARA M346, Catalog No. 2133274, 8.

34. *The War of the Rebellion: A Compilation of the Official Records of the Union and Confederate Armies* (Washington, D.C.: Government Printing Office, 1896) Series I, Vol. IV, 127 (hereafter cited as AOR).

35. Thomas North, *Five Years in Texas; or, What You Did Not Hear During the War from January 1861 to January 1866* (Cincinnati, OH: Elm Street Printing, 1871), 105–06.

36. Alwyn Barr, "Texas Coastal Defense, 1861–1865," in Ralph Wooster (ed.), *Lone Star Blue and Gray: Essays on Texas in the Civil War* (Austin: Texas State Historical Association, 1995), 161.

37. Barr, "Texas Coastal Defense," 161–62; Edward T. Cotham, *Battle on the Bay: The Civil War Struggle for Galveston* (Austin: University of Texas Press, 1998), 63.

38. Chester G. Hearn, *Admiral David Glasgow Farragut: The Civil War Years* (Annapolis, MD: U.S. Naval Institute, 1997), 183–84. Detailed accounts of the Battle of Galveston can be found in Cotham's *Battle on the Bay* and the present author's *The Galveston-Houston Packet: Steamboats on Buffalo Bayou* (The History Press, 2012).

39. Hearn, *Admiral David Glasgow Farragut*, 315; Alfred Thayer Mahan, *Admiral Farragut* (New York: J.A. Hill & Co., 1904), 322.

40. ORN I:19, 745.

41. AOR, I:XV, 1063–64.

42. *Houston Telegraph*, April 6, 1862, 2.

43. Ibid., October 28, 1864, 2.

44. Hayes, *History of the Island and City*, 600–01.

45. Philip C. Tucker III, "The United States Gunboat *Harriet Lane*," *Southwestern Historical Quarterly* 21, no. 4, 372–74.

46. Francis O. Davenport, *On a Man-of-War: A Series of Naval Sketches* (Detroit: E.B. Smith, 1878), 120–21.

47. ORN I:19, 838–40; Cotham, *Battle on the Bay*, 151; Tucker, "United States Gunboat *Harriet Lane*," 374; Cotham, *Battle on the Bay*, 152; Charles S. Davis and J. Barto Arnold III, *Colin J. McRae: Confederate Financial Agent* (College Station, TX: Institute of Nautical Archaeology, 2008), 177.

48. Cotham, *Battle on the Bay*, 170–71; ORN I:21, 911–12.

49. Cotham, *Battle on the Bay*, 171–72; ORN I:21, 44–45; ORN I:21, 138; ORN I:21, 142–43.

50. *Galveston Daily News*, July 15 1874, 3; *[Portland, ME] Daily Eastern Argus*, June 3, 1864, 2.

51. Stephen R. Wise, *Lifeline of the Confederacy: Blockade Running During the Civil War* (Columbia: University of South Carolina Press, 1988), 187–88; Cotham, *Battle of the Bay*, 171–72; ORN I:21, 227–29. Contemporary Union records of this event refer to *Lavinia* by her original name, *Harriet Lane*, and *Alice* by a previous name, *Matagorda*.

52. ORN I:21, 231.

53. *Alexandria Gazette*, May 17, 1864, 1; AOR I:XXXIV, Part 4, 666.

54. *Springfield Daily Illinois State Journal*, January 26, 1865, 3; *Galveston Daily News*, July 15, 1874, 1.

55. *Galveston Tri Weekly Civilian*, November 25, 1872, 1.

56. *Galveston Daily News*, November 27, 1872, 2.

Chapter 5

57. Rodman L. Underwood, *Waters of Discord: The Union Blockade of Texas During the Civil War* (Jefferson, NC: McFarland & Co., 2003), 22.

58. ORN I:16, 654–55.

59. Michael J. Bennett, *Union Jacks: Yankee Sailors in the Civil War* (Chapel Hill: University of North Carolina Press, 2005), 5–7.

60. Bennett, *Union Jacks*, 9.

61. Bennett, *Union Jacks*, 12; Dennis J. Ringle, *Life in Mr. Lincoln's Navy* (Annapolis, MD: Naval Institute Press, 1998), 12; Joseph P. Reidy, "Black Men in Navy Blue During the Civil War," *Prologue: Quarterly of the National Archives and Records Administration* 33, no. 3.

62. Bennett, *Union Jacks*, 159–65.

63. Alfred Thayer Mahan, *From Sail to Steam: Recollections of Naval Life* (New York: Harper & Bros., 1907), 174–75.

64. Davenport, *On a Man-of-War*, 119.

65. Mahan, *From Sail to Steam*, 175.

66. Ringle, *Life in Mr. Lincoln's Navy*, 107–08.

67. Ibid., 118–19.

68. Winfield Scott Schley, *Forty-Five Years Under the Flag* (New York: Appleton, 1904), 31.

69. ORN I:19, 110–11; ibid., I:21, 614–15; ibid., I:20, 407; ibid., I:19, 105, 289; ibid., I:20, 483.

70. World Health Organization, "Yellow Fever," Fact Sheet No. 100, revised December 2001. www.who.int/inf-fs/en/fact100.html.

71. Tom Taylor, *Running the Blockade: A Personal Narrative of Adventures, Risks, and Escapes During the American Civil War* (New York: Charles Scribner's Sons, 1896), 153–54. There were two blockade runners named *Banshee* during the war, both of which became well known. Only the second *Banshee*, though, ran into Texas. To avoid confusion, I've adopted the convention used by Wise in *Lifeline of the Confederacy* and refer to this second ship as *Banshee (II)*.

Chapter 6

72. Marcus W. Price, "Ships That Tested the Blockade of the Gulf Ports," *American Neptune* (1951), 290.

73. Gordon P. Watts Jr., "Phantoms of Anglo-Confederate Commerce: An Historical and Archaeological Investigation of American Civil War Blockade Running" (PhD diss., University of St. Andrews, 1997), 326–27; Eric J. Graham, *Clydebuilt: The Blockade Runners, Cruisers and Armoured Rams of the American Civil War* (Edinburgh: Birlinn, 2006), 185; ibid., 207; ibid., 103. A thorough technical discussion of blockade runner hull design and performance appears in Andrew Wiggins and Sam Ernst, "Civil War Blockade Runners: A Technical History" (BS thesis, Webb Institute, 2003).

74. Watson, *Adventures of a Blockade Runner*, 312. Graham, in *Clydebuilt*, places this incident "late in 1864," but Watson's narrative has it occurring immediately after his run into Galveston in *Pelican*, which can be corroborated in other sources as being near the end of March 1865.

75. Wise, *Lifeline of the Confederacy*, 162.

76. Taylor, *Running the Blockade*, 101–02.

77. Ibid., 105–10.

78. B.H. Carroll, *Standard History of Houston, Texas, from a Study of the Original Sources* (Knoxville, TN: H.W. Crew, 1912), 454.

79. U.S. Census of 1860, Ward 2, Houston, Harris County, Texas, 105.

80. Sylvia Stallings Morris, ed., *William Marsh Rice and His Institute: A Biographical Study* (Houston, TX: Rice University Press, 1972), 30–33.

81. Ibid., 36; Watson, *Adventures of a Blockade Runner*, 26.

82. Morris, *William Marsh Rice*, 36–37.

83. *Galveston Tri-Weekly News*, March 29, 1853, and April 5, 1853; clipping from unknown periodical, April 23, 1853, Galveston and Texas History Center, Rosenberg Library.

84. Godfrey Hodgson, *Woodrow Wilson's Right Hand: The Life of Colonel Edward M. House* (New Haven, CT: Yale University Press, 2006), 17.

85. Ibid., 16–17; Marguerite Johnston, *Houston: The Unknown City, 1836–1946* (College Station: Texas A&M Press, 1991), 67.

86. *Galveston Daily News*, March 19, 1865, 2; *Houston Telegraph*, March 24, 1865; Wise, *Lifeline of the Confederacy*, 315. Wise (in Appendices 17 and 18) lists only one call at Galveston by *Jeanette*, in January 1865, but Watson notes that when he ran her out through the blockade, it was the ship's "second or third trip between Havana and Galveston" (p. 307). Watson

identifies her owner as "Mr. H., a prominent merchant in Houston and Galveston...[who] did much business with the Quartermaster's Department, and most of the goods brought in by blockade runners and bought by that department passed through his hands" (p. 193). "Mr. H." is almost certainly William T. House.

87. Block, *Schooner Sail to Starboard*, 245–46; Hodgson, *Woodrow Wilson's Right Hand*, 17; J.T. Headley, *Our Navy in the Great Rebellion: Heroes and Battles of the War, 1861–65* (New York: E.B. Treat, 1891), 593, 595; Porter, *Naval History of the Civil War*, 840–41.

88. Hodgson, *Woodrow Wilson's Right Hand*, 16.

89. Ibid., 19. Thomas W. House's son Edward Mandell House, whose earliest memories included strolling with his father on the Galveston beach and counting Union blockading ships on the horizon, would later be known as "Colonel" House and serve as a key foreign policy advisor to President Woodrow Wilson.

90. Judith Fenner Gentry, "A Confederate Success in Europe: The Erlanger Loan," *Journal of Southern History* 36, no. 2, 159–60.

91. Ibid., 161–62; Dudley quoted in Wise, *Lifeline of the Confederacy*, 94; Gentry, "Erlanger Loan," 171. Those left holding Erlanger bonds at the end of the war lost their investment. The United States never had any intention of honoring any Confederate bonds or currency and acted quickly after the war to codify that policy into law. One of the provisions of the Fourteenth Amendment to the U.S. Constitution, ratified in 1868, was that "neither the United States nor any State shall assume or pay any debt or obligation incurred in aid of insurrection or rebellion against the United States...All such debts, obligations and claims shall be held illegal and void."

92. Phil Leigh, "The Cotton Bond Bubble," *New York Times* Disunion blog, January 30, 2013.

93. Gerald R. Powell, Matthew C. Cordon and J. Barto Arnold III, *Civil War Blockade Runners: Prize Claims and Historical Record, Including the Denbigh's Court Documents* (College Station, TX: Institute of Nautical Archaeology, 2012), 121–26.

94. D.W. Harris, *Maritime History of Thyl and Rhuddlan* (Clwyd, UK: Books Prints & Pictures, 1991), 22–24; *Liverpool Register Book*, entry no. 198 for 1860, Merseyside Maritime Museum, Liverpool. Laird's reputation for iron shipbuilding was such in the 1860s that when Jules Verne published his famous novel *20,000 Leagues Under the Sea*, he had Captain Nemo explain to Professor Aronnax that he had spared no expense in building *Nautilus*, using hull plating custom-ordered from Laird.

95. *Lloyd's Captains' Register, Containing the Names of Certificated Masters of the British Mercantile Marine, Now Afloat* (London: Committee for Managing the Affairs of Lloyd's, 1869); "Agreement and Account of Crew Foreign-Going Ship," October 15, 1863, Public Record Office, London.
96. Thomas Dudley, "Report on the Suspected Blockade Runner *Denbigh*," October 1863. *Denbigh* file, Stephen R. Wise Collection, Parris Island, South Carolina.

CHAPTER 7

97. Davenport, *On a Man-of-War*, 78.
98. Library of Congress, "A Bill for the Better Government of the Navy of the United States, and Repealing and Act on the Same Subject, Passed the Second Day of March in the Year One Thousand Seven Hundred and Ninety-nine," March 3, 1800; Underwood, *Waters of Discord*, 35.
99. Underwood, *Waters of Discord*, 35; Watts Jr., "Phantoms of Anglo-Confederate Commerce," 87; Symonds, *Lincoln and His Admirals*, 307.
100. Symonds, *Lincoln and His Admirals*, 284–85.
101. ORN I:21, 200; Headley, *Our Navy in the Great Rebellion*, 586; Porter, *Naval History of the Civil War*, 837.
102. ORN I:21, 237, 239.
103. Porter, *Naval History of the Civil War*, 834, 837.
104. ORN I:21, 306; *Houston Telegraph*, June 24, 1864, 4. USS *Admiral* was renamed *Fort Morgan* not long after this incident.
105. ORN I:21, 305–06.
106. *Daily True Delta [New Orleans]*, August 20, 1864, 3; ibid., November 29, 1864, 2; ORN I:21, 309–10.
107. ORN I:21, 351.
108. ORN I:20, 486; Underwood, *Waters of Discord*, 36–37.

Chapter 8

109. AOR 2:VII, 56.

110. Wise, *Lifeline of the Confederacy*, 272; ORN I:21, 330; ORN I:17, 750; ORN I:21, 334–35; ORN I:21, 359.

111. Watson, *Adventures of a Blockade Runner*, 304.

112. Taylor, *Running the Blockade*, 110–11; Wise, *Lifeline of the Confederacy*, 327.

113. *Galveston Tri-Weekly News*, February 8, 1865, 1. The published letter is signed "O. Godfrey," which is almost certainly a garbling of "A. Godfrey." The letter's author is clearly an experienced Gulf blockade-running officer, who mentions his family living in Havana at the time.

114. *Galveston Tri-Weekly News*, February 8, 1865, 1.

115. William A. Ward, "The Saga of the *Will o' the Wisp*, the Story of a Confederate Blockade Runner, Part Three: The *Wisp*'s Last Voyage," *InBetween Magazine*, December 1983, Sec. 2, 3.

116. ORN I:22, 36.

117. Ibid., 34.

118. Hayes, *History of the Island and City*, 630; *Houston Tri-Weekly Telegraph*, February 22, 1865, 4.

119. Frank Hole, "The *Acadia*: A Civil War Blockade Runner." Report to the State of Texas Antiquities Committee, August 1974, Appendix 1.

120. Ibid., 8.

121. *Galveston Weekly News*, March 1, 1865, 1; ORN I:22, 32.

122. *Houston Tri-Weekly Telegraph*, February 20, 1865, 4; *Galveston Weekly News*, February 22, 1865, 2.

123. *Galveston Weekly News*, February 15, 1865, 1.

124. Wise, *Lifeline of the Confederacy*, 290.

125. Taylor, *Running the Blockade*, 151.

126. Ibid., 152–54.

127. Ibid., 156.

128. Ibid., 156-57; *[Atchison, KS] Weekly Champion and Press*, April 27, 1865, 1.

129. Wise, *Lifeline of the Confederacy*, Appendix 17.

130. Watson, *Adventures of a Blockade Runner*, 289–90; Wise, *Lifeline of the Confederacy*, 315. In his memoir, Watson gives this vessel's name as *Phoenix*, but no steamship of that name is known to have run the blockade. Watson's description of the vessel and its voyage closely matches the runner *Pelican*, and David Asprey, a researcher in the United Kingdom, was able to reconstruct *Pelican*'s activities in late 1864 and early 1865 using

Lloyd's List (a daily newspaper) and the *Annual Index of Ship Movements* in Lloyd's Collection, Guildhall Library, London. The details of *Pelican's* career match Watson's description of *Phoenix* very closely, including the description of the ship as a screw steamer (there was only one known to have run into Galveston during that period), as well as her arrival at Havana from London in January and a change of masters shortly before running the blockade.

131. Watson, *Adventures of a Blockade Runner*, 291.

132. Ibid., 292–93.

133. Ibid., 295–99.

134. Ibid., 301–02.

135. ORN I:13, 793.

136. *Galveston Weekly News*, April 14, 1865, 3.

137. John F. Mackie, "Running the Blockade—Escape of the *Fox*," in C.R. Graham (ed.), *Under Both Flags: A Panorama of the Great Civil War* (Baltimore, MD: Veteran Publishing Co., 1896), 329.

138. Ibid., 330.

139. Ibid., 330–31.

140. Ibid., 331.

141. Ibid.

142. *Galveston Weekly News*, April 14, 1865, 3.

143. Mackie, "Running the Blockade," 332.

144. *Mobile Register*, February 12, 1863, 1.

145. Watts Jr., "Phantoms of Anglo-Confederate Commerce," 194.

146. *Galveston Daily News*, April 19, 1865, 2.

147. Ibid.

148. Emma Martin Maffitt, *The Life and Services of John Newland Maffitt* (New York: Neale Publishing, 1906), 350. Emma Maffitt's inaccurate story of *Owl* being stranded under fire from Federal blockaders has been repeated in recent years in Royce Shingleton's *High Seas Confederate: The Life and Times of John Newland Maffitt* (Columbia: University of South Carolina Press, 1994), 97, and in Bland Simpson's *Two Captains from Carolina: Moses Grandy, John Newland Maffitt, and the Coming of the Civil War* (Chapel Hill: University of North Carolina Press, 2012), 162.

CHAPTER 9

149. Wise, *Lifeline of the Confederacy* 294–95; Benjamin F. Sands, *From Reefer to Rear Admiral: Reminiscences and Journal Jottings of Nearly Half a Century of Naval Life* (New York: Frederick A. Stokes, 1899), 277.

150. Hayes, *History of the Island and City*, 600–01.

151. Valuable works on conditions in Galveston for both soldiers and civilians during the war include Schmidt's *Galveston and the Civil War* and Cotham's *Battle on the Bay*.

152. Cotham, *Battle on the Bay*, 154–55.

153. Ibid.,164–65.

154. *Houston Daily Telegraph*, March 8, 1864, 1.

155. Ralph J. Smith, "Reminiscences of Life on the Gulf Coast with the Second Texas Infantry," in B.P. Gallaway (ed.), *Texas: The Dark Corner of the Confederacy* (Lincoln: University of Nebraska, 1994), 191; Cotham, *Battle on the Bay*, 162–64.

156. Cotham, *Battle on the Bay*, 178.

157. Wise, *Lifeline of the Confederacy*, Appendix 17, 273.

158. ORN I:22, 197.

159. Wise, *Lifeline of the Confederacy*, 219.

160. Watson, *Adventures of a Blockade Runner*, 287–88.

161. *Galveston Daily News*, May 28, 1891, 9; Cotham, *Battle on the Bay*, 179; Wise, *Lifeline of the Confederacy* Appendix 18, 275; ibid., 219.

162. Sands, *From Reefer to Rear Admiral*, 272–73; Robert L. Kerby, *Kirby Smith's Confederacy: The Trans-Mississippi South, 1863–1865* (Tuscaloosa: University of Alabama Press, 1972), 423–24.

163. Sands, *From Reefer to Rear Admiral*, 276–77; Kerby, *Kirby Smith's Confederacy*, 426. A handful of other small, isolated Confederate units surrendered after June 2, but the Trans-Mississippi Department, which encompassed Missouri, Arkansas, Texas, Indian Territory and Louisiana west of the Mississippi River, was the last major command of the Confederacy to capitulate.

164. Hayes, *History of the Island and City*, 640–41; Sands, *From Reefer to Rear Admiral*, 277–78.

Epilogue

165. Andrew Johnson, "Proclamation 141—Raising the Blockade of All Ports in the United States Including Galveston, Texas," June 23, 1865. Online by Gerhard Peters and John T. Woolley, the American Presidency Project. www.presidency.ucsb.edu/ws/?pid=71969.

166. Frank Hole, "*Acadia*," 1–3. Unless otherwise cited, all material in this discussion of the salvage of *Acadia* is drawn from Dr. Hole's report.

167. J. Barto Arnold, e-mail message to author, January 31, 2014. See Watson and Arnold, *Civil War Adventures of a Blockade Runner*; Block and Arnold, *Schooner Sail to Starboard*; Davis and Arnold, *Colin J. McRae*; Arnold, *The Denbigh's Civilian Imports: Customs Records of a Civil War Blockade Runner between Mobile and Havana*; Nichols and Arnold, *Confederate Quartermaster in the Trans-Mississippi*; and Powell, Cordon and Arnold, *Civil War Blockade Runners: Prize Claims and the Historical Record*.

168. *InBetween Magazine*, "The Saga of the *Will o' the Wisp*: The Story of a Confederate Blockade Runner, Part One," November 1983, Sec. 2, 1.

169. Ibid., 2.

170. Ibid.

171. Leigh Jones and Rhiannon Meyers, *Infinite Monster: Courage, Hope and Resurrection in the Face of One of America's Largest Hurricanes* (Dallas, TX: PenlandScott, 2010), 107, 128.

INDEX

Y

ABOUT THE AUTHOR

A ndy Hall is a native of the Texas Gulf Coast and a longtime researcher and author, specializing in local maritime and Civil War history. Working with the Texas Historical Commission, the Institute of Nautical Archaeology, the PAST Foundation and other groups, Hall has had the opportunity to help archaeologists record multiple historical shipwrecks, including the famous blockade runners *Denbigh* and *Will o' the Wisp* and the blockaders USS *Arkansas* and USS *Hatteras*.

www.ingramcontent.com/pod-product-compliance
Lightning Source LLC
Chambersburg PA
CBHW060806100426
42813CB00004B/960